D0463854

COME OUT, COME OUT, WHEREVER YOU ARE.

CAROLE SHAW
& Hank Nuwer

American R.R. Publishing Company, Los Angeles

Library of Congress Cataloging in Publication Data
First Edition
Shaw, Carole:
   Come Out, Come Out, Wherever You Are.

To all our great models — Thank You.

B. Courtenay Leigh (pages 16, 33, 34, 70, 83, 92, 93, 142, 143, 153, 163, 165, 166, 167, 169, 196, 203, 235), Conni Peach (pages 17, 33, 35, 62, 65, 77, 85, 88, 99, 108, 124, 150, 152, 227), Idrea (pages 33, 34, 92, 102, 125, 137, 140, 188, 221, 240), Joette La Fond (pages 68, 77, 81, 83, 105, 124, 135, 159, 172, 196), Gloria Mushonga (pages 148, 151, 237, Carol Ann (page 196), Wossenu (pages 17, 219), Bonnie McClain (pages 211, 234), Helen Lipton (page 225), Saundra Zagaria (page 219), Mary Duffy (page 229), Sherry Staab (page 229), Sandra Perry (page 183), Allison Gappa (page 133), Mar (page 229), Jason Carr (page 93), Amy De Vore (page 188), Peter Rasi (page 62). Ray Vas (page 85), Doe Harris (page 16),Roseanna Lee (page 206), Cleverley Stone (page 244), Linda Richardson (page 92), Berta Barhes (page 92), Randy Furhman (page 92), Armando Chaparro (page 92), Albert Nunez (page 92), Cindy Michaels (page 92)

Our thanks too:
To all the fine photographers whose pictures appeared on these pages.

Nancy Santullo, Cover Photo
Steven Ohanesian (pages 16, 148, 196, 219, 227, 235), Brigitte Wiltzer (pages 17, 108, 124, 125, 151, 152, 179, 221, 237), Bob Abrams (pages 34, 172, 206), Donald Sanders (pages 33, 34, 35), Peter Kredenser (pages 62, 65, 68, 70, 77, 81, 83, 88, 105, 137), Patti Lotz (pages 85, 92, 102, 203), Bob Shad (page 45), Kenneth Bank (pages 93, 140, 159, 225), Henry Schwartze (pages 92, 219), Kay Shuper (pages 22, 133, 150), Schift (page 16), Mark Brett (pages 129-131), Robert Tyck (page 211), Jeanette Korab (229), Richard Cartwright (page 229), James Mores (page 183), Melody Thamar Saunders (page 188), Edward Levine (pages 142, 143, 153, 163, 165, 166, 169), Roxanne Rifken (page 135).

ISBN: 0-910277-001

DEDICATION

To my husband Ray,
   Heart of my life—
And our daughters
   Lori and Victoria,
Joy of our hearts.
And to BBWs all over the world
   Who have stepped out from behind themselves.

ACKNOWLEDGEMENTS

To Ray, who supplied the sushi and the love.

To Cheri Weismantel who worked and worried and typed her fingers to the bone and who can probably recite this book by heart.

To Bob Cohen who put on our doggie door so I could concentrate on writing.

To Jenine Nuwer, Hank's wife, for her patience and help.

To Selene Garrett for her help.

To my brother Lenny who is still thin.

To my Mother and Father who made this possible.

CONTENTS

WARNING : : :

This is a SURVIVAL GUIDE for the big woman. It is *not* a "get slim" or "how to look thinner" fashion book. If you want that kind of information, I can direct you to a myriad of books which will give you morning exercise regimens and tell you what length your skirt should be.

What I don't want to do is to change your body shape. What I want to do is change your mind shape.

As a big woman I know where it hurts—and so do you. If you've never hurt there, then please write your own book and share your secrets with us!

I'm not going to spell out the problems. We know the problem by heart, and it has nothing to do with eye shadow or morning exercises.

You are all diet veterans so I won't bore you with basics of good nutrition. I assume that we all know the basics. I'm going to talk to you about where your head should be when confronted with rules, regulations and prejudice about your size.

In my heart of hearts I care not whether you choose to lose or gain or maintain the status quo, or if you ultimately belt your dress. I care only that for the first time you will understand and give yourself permission to make a choice about your size. *Your* choice. *Not* mine or some so-called expert's.

That which is *you* has nothing to do with weight. Remember that in one hundred years, all of us are going to weigh the same! Once you convince yourself that this is so—no one again will depress you over the issue of weight.

This book deals with common sense solutions to the *other* guy's problem with our weight. I'm not advocating any rash or radical behavior. I don't want you to go out and put on 50 additional pounds next month, or to even be a half-ounce heavier than what makes you feel good and comfortable. That would be putting my pressure on you, just the way the "thin is in" advocates have done to us.

There are always two ways of looking at a thing. You can look at your glass and say it is half-empty or half-full. You can look at a doughnut and see the circle or the hole. You can look at yourself in the mirror and see a fat person, or you can, as I do, look into the mirror and see a big person who is also beautiful.

If there is only one thing you get out of my book, it is that you can give yourself permission to be big *and* beautiful. My philosophy is a philosophy of self-love. Fat is not where it's at. Thin is not where it's at. Medium is not where it's at. *Alive is where it's at!*

If you ask me whether I'd rather be fat or skinny, I'll tell you I'd rather be *alive and happy*. You only have two choices in this life. You can love yourself or you can hate yourself. So which is it going to be? What is the *only* choice that makes sense? If you're happy and content in your heart, you'll be surprised how happy and content the hearts around you will be too. Fat is not the issue. Living is the issue.

The only issue.

In other words, follow your own direction where weight is concerned. My direction is not necessarily yours, but maybe the direction of some hotshot dress designer is not yours, either. Be good to yourself. You're the best friend you'll ever have. Can you really afford to make an enemy out of someone as close to you as yourself?

GETTING PERSONAL : : :

I weigh 200 lbs., more soaking wet.

I am a big woman living in a world obsessed with thinness. I am soft and round in a world gone mad for protruding bones and angles. For over thirty years I dieted and succeeded many, many times in losing weight. (If that ache in my midsection could be called success!) For brief periods of time I was among the hallowed ranks of the fashionably thin. ALMOST.

Surprisingly, slimming down didn't change anything about my life. No one made a size nine statue of me to place in Central Park. But it did do one thing for me, it made me hungry and depressed. Hungry—because cottage cheese, yogurt and tuna packed in water was not my idea of a satisfying menu. Depressed—because this kind of awful deprivation was like being sentenced to prison . . . and sooner or later I knew I'd break out.

IT PAYS TO ASK

One day, as I prepared to begin still another diet, I asked myself an amazing question:

WHY?

Why what?

WHY AM I DOING THIS TO MYSELF?

To be thin.

WHY?

Because I'm *supposed* to be thin.

WHY?

Because *everyone else* tells everyone they're supposed to be thin.

WHY?

———

WHY?

———

I don't know!!!!!!

11

Not exactly a dialogue out of Shakespeare, but for me the revelation was certainly *The Tempest*. I had never questioned myself about my dieting before.

(Here comes the "heavy" part!) I STOPPED DIETING, and I entered a hitherto unthinkable and unexplored world—or at least a world that had been a ghost town since Victorian times—the world of BBW: BIG BEAUTIFUL WOMAN.

Welcome to it!

BBW

I am the editor of a fashion magazine called *BBW: Big Beautiful Woman*, dedicated to the premise that big women are created equal to every other woman, size notwithstanding.

What *BBW Magazine* is helping to change is the American prejudice that fat is synonymous with ugly.

I'm a big lady. You can call me a fat lady. I don't mind so long as your tone of voice is objective instead of inflammatory. Fat is not a dirty word. I see the word "fat" as a classification. If I said to Clint Eastwood: "You're a tall man," he wouldn't be insulted. It's just a way of classifying him according to physical *appearance*. He *is* a *tall* man, just as I am a *fat* lady. One weight isn't right for everybody, just as one nose isn't right for everybody—just as one diet isn't right for everybody. God made St. Bernards, and he also made Chihuahuas. There's room for all of us, be we Cadillac or Toyota, king-size or compacts. When are lovehandles bad? Only when no one fondles them.

NOTHING BUT THE BEST

This book isn't only for "fat people." It is for every person who ever cried into her pillow about the way she looks, including the skinny woman who feels she's too flat chested and the woman who believes she is "over the hill" because she doesn't look like the 15-year-old on the cover of Vogue. Size is no guarantee of happiness—neither is youth or wealth or good looks. If the major thing standing between you and happiness right now is a little weight, be prepared to take that weight off from the only place it *really* counts. Off your shoulders.

It is my plan that when you finish this book, you will:

A. STOP FEELING GUILTY about your size and concentrate on developing the attractive, wonderful person you already are. You are a unique individual worthy of being loved and fully understood. Moreover, you have done nothing wrong.

B. STOP LIVING FOR OTHERS. If you have always dieted in the belief that others will think more highly of you, consider this: Are you any smarter if you wear a size eight dress? Do you earn a presidential commendation if you drop 80 lbs. in six weeks? Are your neighbors necessarily impressed because you're the first one on the block with a dead bolt on the fridge?

C. STOP MEASURING YOUR WORTH BY YOUR DRESS SIZE. You don't become less of a person by taking up more space. Because you are big does not make you more or less educated, informed or (Ho, Ho!) jollier. Beauty comes in all sizes. While you have no right to ask someone else to kiss your ring upon meeting you, neither must you tolerate being treated like a second class citizen by *anyone* of *any* size simply because *they* are pound foolish. Refuse to accept less than first class treatment in any area of your life.

D. STOP BUYING INFERIOR, ILL-DESIGNED AND ILL-MADE CLOTHES. Believing that desirability stops when a woman reaches size 18, the fashion industry too long has offered us inferior merchandise. We've also been taken for a ride by the media, the medical profession, the travel industry, beauticians and society in general. But now that we are at last making it clear we are mad as hell and taking it no longer, the future looks bright for the millions of us who do not equate a double chin with terminal illness.

Large size is no guarantee of unhappiness. As with skinny persons, sometimes a fat person is happy, sometimes sad. My aim is to reduce a bit of the world's sadness by helping anyone whose main source of despair is his or her weight.

In writing this book my uppermost thought was not to tell anybody "how to" do anything, so much as "how *not* to" do certain things. Like how not to be intimidated. Like how not to follow the crowd. Like how not to get down on yourself.

If there is a "how to" that I endorse, however, it is how to love yourself.

What I would like to do is to put this whole obsession with size back into perspective. No matter how *big* we are, it's only a *small* portion of *what* we are and can accomplish. So let's get on with living our lives.

WHO ARE WE ANYWAY?

There are 30 million women size 16 or larger in the United States. That's one out of every three adult women. So you see, it's not just you, me and 12 other crazy ladies!

Big women tend to feel very isolated. Most all the women we ever see in movies, magazines, newspapers or on television are thin. When we walk down the street we never seem to see the other larger-size lady. We only seem to see the size nine. We sometimes get the feeling we are the only big woman in the world. However, a close look at the accompanying statistics will give you a better idea of the company you share.

GETTING IT ALL TOGETHER

Since fully 30 percent of the adult female population are size 16 or larger—with millions of us earning substantial sums of money—we Big Beautiful Women have clout if we unite to use it. Some crude people might call this movement Fat Power, but certainly we are not to be ignored or ridiculed ever again. By taking ourselves seriously, others will take us the same way.

We do not advocate anyone gain one pound *more* than they are happy and healthy with, but we *insist* no one need weigh one pound *less*, either.

One thing is certain. We don't have to come out of any closet. Big people have always been visible. It's just time we make an impact by putting our collective foot down.

My aim is to help you make your life happier by coaching you in these pages on how to best use everything you've got. And what you've got is *you*—you in all your potential glamour and glory.

Let this book act as a testimony to the fact we will from this time forward refuse to accept anything less than a full slice of life! Or put another way: Life is *not* over for the overweight. Amen.

A PROFILE OF THE BBW

AGE*

40%   25 to 35 years old
35%   35 to 50 years old
*75%   Between 25 and 50 years old.
The most active period of a
person's life.

MARITAL STATUS

54%   Married
25%   Single
15%   Divorced
2%   Separated
20%   No children
50%   1 - 2 Children
29%   3 or more children

EDUCATION*

41%   Some College
15%   College graduates
16%   Post-graduate
31%   College graduates
27%   High School graduates
*We are well educated

OCCUPATION*

30%   Executive/Managerial/
Professional
19%   Secretaries and Clerks
17%   Housewives (exclusively)
*Majority are working women

SALARY RANGE*

30% $10,000/$20,000 per year
30% $20,000/$35,000 per year
15% $35,000 and up
*We are affluent
62%   Live in a house (of which
50% are owners not renters)
50%   Own 1, 2 or more cars

TYPES OF ACTIVITIES WE ENJOY

75%   Travel   52%   Theatre
80%   Music   48%   Sewing
83%   Reading   48%   Entertaining

We tend to be cultured, artistic, active,
community-minded women

In the last 12 months:

65%   attended a theatre
production
55%   visited an art museum or
gallery
44%   attended a concert, opera or
symphony
37%   took an adult education
course
48%   participated in community or
civic affairs

LIFE STYLE*

56%   dine out 4 or more times per
month
40%   entertain at home 2 or more
times per month
43%   take one vacation per year
44%   take 2 or more vacations per
year
54%   spend 2 or more weeks
vacationing per year
*We are a very social and active group
of women.

15

Myth:

FATANDUGLY IS ONE WORD.

False.

It ain't what you got, it's what you do with it.

1 | FROM RUSSIA WITH LOVEHANDLES

Following in the great tradition of Dostoyevsky, Pasternak and Tolstoi, my story opens in a small Russian peasant village. That's where my mother was born and raised. The story of how she lived is the history of how I came to be.

Until she was six, my mother lived in a very poor Russian village named Streshen. It was much like Tevya's birthplace in *Fiddler on the Roof*, a collection of wind-buffeted homes situated along the banks of the Dniper River. She never, never forgot what it was like to be hungry and to eat black bread for supper, followed by more black bread for dessert.

My mother was a tiny, thin child who after coming to America's land-of-plenty grew up nevertheless to be a tiny, thin woman. Only 5′ tall—though she lied and claimed an extra inch—her vision of the good life was to have a great round face. To her that meant health, life and vitality.

Not surprisingly, she married a strapping six footer whose most evident feature was a round moon-face. They sired two children: my brother Lenny and me.

Poor Lenny! His entire childhood was spent being dragged off to doctors because he was skinny as a beanpole. Mother used to pay *him* to eat, but she never had to offer me a cent. No wonder he retired at 43, and I'm still working.

One of my clearest memories is of Lenny coming home from school, and my mother waiting to ambush him with a special appetite-inducing tonic the doctor had prescribed. He *hated* that tonic. My mother used to chase him in and out of closets and under beds to get him to take it.

"What is so terrible?" she always screamed at him.

One day he screamed back. *"You* try it!" My mother took one spoonful and flung the bottle right out the window.

On the other hand there was me. It pleased my mother to no end to have one robust child. She thought it was just wonderful that I looked like a plump cupcake. In fact my mother used to say that Jackie Gleason stole his favorite line from her. When I was young she delighted in pinching my cheek and squealing "How swee—eee—eeet it is!"

So there we were, my brother and I, sitting at the same table and eating the same meals that Mother prepared. He stayed skinny as a rail, and I became a tiny Russian woman's dream—a big beautiful girl.

But since I grew up in America, not in Russia, I never saw myself the way my mother did. Obsessed with a Hollywood vision of what a woman should look like, I considered myself fat. It was no fun to go to summer camp and come home with all my own clothes because no one else could wear my size! I used to spend my life in terror of a chocolate chip cookie. Every morning when I awoke, I never knew if the day had dawned good or bad until I stepped onto a scale.

But what is fat, anyway? You'd have to be some kind of a genius to define the term. Calvin Klein probably thinks that anyone who can't slither into size six jeans is obese, and a supposedly chic creep of a boutique owner named Fiorucci insists that no one over a size ten has any reason to be alive. People like these two self-esteemed gents believe that big women can enjoy nothing in life and deserve less! Then there's the doctor who dictates that if you can "pinch an inch" of midriff, you are overweight.

But when someone tells me now that I'm overweight, I always say "Over *whose* weight?" I'm not over *my* weight; this *is* my weight. Maybe I'm over *your* weight! It's like saying that I am over-age. How can I be over-age when this *is* my age?

For that matter, the actual pound total of what I weigh is irrelevant to what I am as a human being. No matter what the scale reads, I am a valuable, worthwhile person, and this is true whether I gain or lose pounds.

SUNNY SIDE UP

I have a friend named Sunny. Although she quit school two months before her high school graduation, she is the smartest person that I know personally. She taught me one important piece of advice. Before agonizing over a "should I or shouldn't I" situation and finding yourself at an impossible impasse, ask yourself instead, *"What's the worst thing that could happen?"* Sunny taught me to face my demons directly, and this, many times, helped me take the terror out of a conflict. I've found that the anticipation of an impending disaster is often worse than the disaster itself.

I'd like *you* to take Sunny's advice for a moment and think about your weight. *What's the worst thing that could happen?* The "worst" thing is that you'll be fat.

And now that you've said it, here's another news flash. We may be fat, but we are *not* ugly.

HEAVY MATTERS

With all the pressure exerted on us from every direction, why is it that there are so many fat people anyway? Isn't it time we drew back for a moment to examine society's "rules" and question whether they are right for everyone? Contrary to what the diet industry would have you believe, fat people are not sick, and though some of us *may* be sick, it's not always fat that makes us sick. A goodly portion of this sickness may be because we've been forced to deal with incredible social and psychological stress connected with our weight.

While I have been known to poke fun at dieting for fashion's sake alone, if you have a definite illness such as heart trouble, diabetes, hypoglycemia and so on, *please* do yourself a favor and diet. In that case you are dieting because you love yourself, and you love life too much to leave it. Remember that is exactly what this book is about: a love of life.

But if you are a big healthy woman, I'd like you to examine your life. Don't you resent being manipulated by the multi-million dollar fashion and diet industry? I do. I resent it for me, and I resent it for my children. We have the power to say "Nay!" to all this thinomania madness. We must learn how to say "no" to those who oppress us.

We've foolishly gone along with the perpetrators of crimes against us, those people who believe fat people deserve all the "no's" they get. You must start with yourself to halt this unhealthy trend. Say *no* to self-hate and self-denial inflicted upon yourself in the name of a fashionable waistline. Say *yes* to life, and get on with the business of living.

If you don't live your life now, when will you live it? Don't think the mortician will let you run out for one last piece of fresh cheesecake!!!

THE INESTIMABLE BRUCE

When I was 11, a friend promised me an introduction to a boy called Bruce. Now that might not seem an earthshaking event to you, but coming from New York's earthy Lower East Side, the name "Bruce" conjured up images of inestimable romance and eternal bliss. How can I tell you what the name Bruce did to me. Bruce was like saying "Lancelot" or "Tristan." I had never even heard the name Bruce before, let alone had the privilege of meeting one. If at that time every little breeze seemed to whisper Louise, then every little spruce was shouting out *Bruce!*

Unfortunately, right before I was to meet this boy, I heard a hit song on the radio by Arthur Godfrey that made me want to hide in my room and never come out. The song began with the words: "I don't want her, you can have her; she's too fat for me!" In my little girl heart-of-hearts I knew that those lyrics had been written after the writer had seen *me* personally on the street. I was 5'4", and weighed all of 140 lbs. If a *songwriter* wouldn't want me because I was too fat, what chance did I have with Bruce? I wanted to be Cinderella with Bruce as the Prince Charming. Then I found out I couldn't fit into Cinderella's dress!

Since the introduction was already fated, I resolved to attempt one brave effort to win the lad's undying affection. Collecting all my savings, I went shopping. After hours of feet-killing search, I located a green skirt and a Gibson Girl blouse with sleeves that puffed out like mushroom caps, the latest rage in 1947. To make me look thinner I also purchased a girdle, a contraption with steel stays no doubt invented by some nefarious genius of sadistic torture.

MAMA'S BIG, LITTLE GIRL

That afternoon I showed my purchases to my mother, ever mindful that having known starvation in her native Russia, her daily prayer was for a full belly, not a tiny behind.

"You don't need a girdle," my mother said patiently to me.

"No?"

"What you need is exercise."

I looked at my mother in dismay. Jogging along the old neighborhood's streets was an invitation to a mugging. Only the purse snatchers were in shape.

"How can I get any exercise here!" I wailed.

My mother mulled the problem over for a few minutes and then told me about a fabled Russian queen who wasn't allowed to leave the palace. She exercised by throwing shredded paper all over the floor and stooping to pick it up piece-by-piece.

Although skeptical, I followed her suggestion faithfully each day, looking ever so forlornly like one of the bentbacked reapers in that painting by Millet.

The experiment, unfortunately, failed miserably. Not only did I not lose weight, but I developed a paranoia about attending weddings. I had visions of my diving headlong over the bride's train to gather up confetti out of some perverse Pavlovian reflex.

Years later, when I had developed severe back trouble, I often thought about the incomparable Bruce.

I wanted to send *him* the chiropractor bill!

Oh, by the way! If anyone is interested in what happened with Bruce—he was a very nice boy, and we got along fine—but he lived in the Bronx, a good hour subway ride away. So in the end, it wasn't my weight that ended our romance, it was the New York subway system. Well, what the heck, I was only 11.

A FOOTSOLDIER IN THE WAR AGAINST FAT

The point of the story is that I've always been a footsoldier in the war against fat. I believed all the propaganda spewed out everywhere in books, magazines and the cinema. Fat was ugly. "Everyone" seemed to know that, and certainly I knew of no Prince Charming who had fallen for a fat princess.

For years and years and years I bought the bill of goods against fat, propagated initially no doubt by someone who really didn't like women very much. It took me years to learn one valuable concept: *No matter what I weigh, no matter what you weigh, no matter what anyone weighs, we are all valuable, worthwhile people, capable of loving and receiving love in return.*

23

At age four I was a tiny Russian woman's dream.

My mother said that I was born hungry.

My father: 6' tall and 250 lbs.

Brother Lenny: 6' tall and 130 lbs.

Mother, my Uncle Ben and me in my WACs outfit (age six). Notice how nicely my jacket doesn't close.

That's me in the middle at eight years old. Guess who I take after.

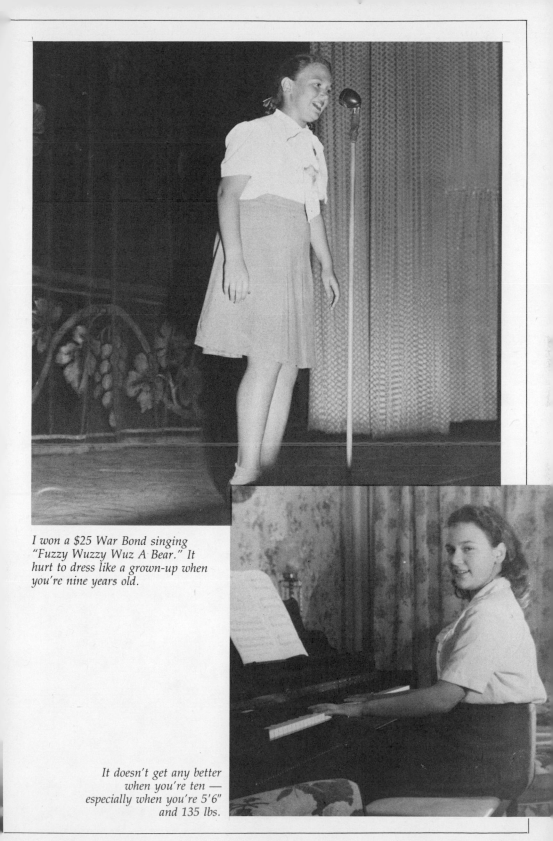

I won a $25 War Bond singing "Fuzzy Wuzzy Wuz A Bear." It hurt to dress like a grown-up when you're nine years old.

It doesn't get any better when you're ten — especially when you're 5'6" and 135 lbs.

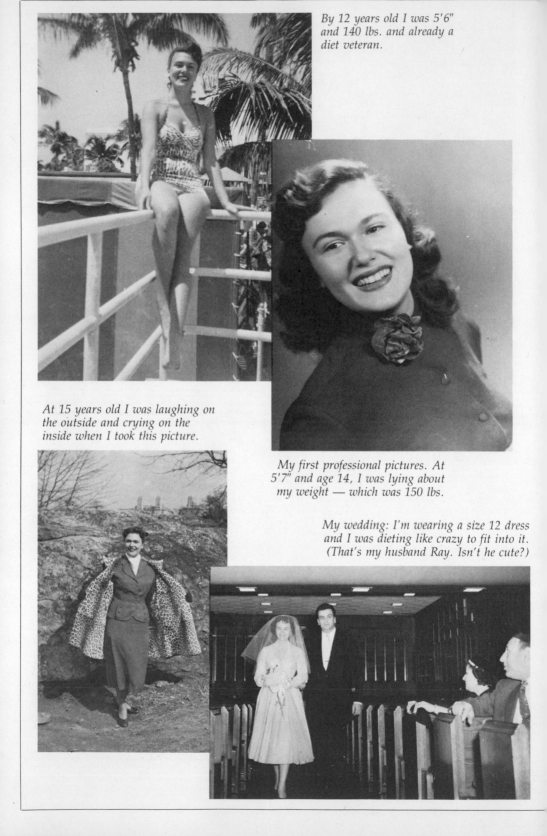

By 12 years old I was 5'6" and 140 lbs. and already a diet veteran.

At 15 years old I was laughing on the outside and crying on the inside when I took this picture.

My first professional pictures. At 5'7" and age 14, I was lying about my weight — which was 150 lbs.

My wedding: I'm wearing a size 12 dress and I was dieting like crazy to fit into it. (That's my husband Ray. Isn't he cute?)

I'm in showbiz and obsessed with looking thinner than my 150 lbs. With all my dieting do you see the lovehandles?

So put aside your guilt. Better yet, bury it forever. You have done nothing to feel guilty about. Have you ever strangled an insensitive Gucci salesgirl with your pantihose or threatened a diet panderer with evisceration? Have you ever, however deserved, beat senseless your tasteless cousin from Hoboken who has a thing for fat jokes? Of course you haven't. So let the guilt stop here and now.

Think about it. Are you any smarter in a size eight dress than in a size 18 or a size 48? Is your basic character more worthwhile at 120 lbs. than at 220? Is there a swinging gate in heaven which measures your hips before you're allowed inside?

Who you are and what you are has nothing to do with your circumference. You are not necessarily a better or more successful person if you are skinny. Slim people apply for food stamps, too.

The idea is to use a little common sense. Don't accept popular notions about weight just because you are surrounded—even suffocated—by them. Then see if maybe, just maybe, all the fears and complications that have snarled up your life because of fat are based upon groundless, mindless assumptions and myths.

BEAUTY ONLY THIN-SKIN DEEP?

Who decides what is sexy? A few so-called geniuses in Hollywood and the fashion centers of the world. Today, based on entertainment guidelines for star sizes, Raquel Welch wouldn't even be offered a screen test. And the old calendar sensation herself, Betty Grable, would never get her thighs on a Playboy centerfold this year. Hugh Hefner probably would say they were too fat.

POUND FOOLISH

About six months ago I walked into the foyer at BBW and saw a gorgeous girl sitting there. "Gee, you sure are beautiful," I said. I couldn't get over how great she looked, but my compliment only embarassed her. She had come to model for BBW because it was fun to be featured in a national magazine, but still, she confessed, her dream was to appear in a svelte model's publication such as *Cosmo*. Even though right now she was a *perfect* large-size model figure, she confided that she was on a diet.

"What's wrong with you?" I asked in amazement.

"Well," she said, averting her eyes, "I weigh 185."

"Yes . . . and you look terrific!"

"But I weigh a hundred and eighty-five pounds."

"Have you looked in the mirror deeply and seen how truly attractive you are?" I asked. "Your face, your figure! Everything is in proportion. So why do you have to diet?"

"Because . . . I . . . weigh. . . ."

"—Hold it, hold it!" I said. "Tell me just one thing. If you got on your scale, looking exactly the same as you look this minute except that the scale read 140 lbs., would you be happy?"

"Yes," she said. "Absolutely."

Get the picture? She continued to fall victim to the tyranny of numbers on a scale.

What about *you*? You've got a brain in that big beautiful body. Why not put your scale away for a day, a month, or a lifetime and really look at yourself in the mirror instead? Start getting in touch with your own body. If your body says it does or doesn't feel good, listen to it. It knows what's what.

Why be programmed by a scale? It's only an instrument, for Pete's sake. You're not a piece of meat or a gold bullion bar that is worth more or less depending on your weight. Why decide to hate yourself based—*not* on how you feel, how successful you are, on how you enjoy life—but on what three tiny numbers at your feet say each day? Aren't you beginning to see something is wrong with that kind of logic? Tell me *that* isn't sick.

CHART FOR CHART'S SAKE

To show the fallacy behind relying on pounds as a basis for determining whether one is fat or not, we need only to look to the height-weight charts pawned off on the gullible American public for years by the insurance industry.

When these charts first came out, they were based only on surveys taken of men and women who were insurance policy holders. It took some time for the concept of insurance to catch on, and the first policy holders were basically affluent, conservative people who could afford the premiums. Many bought insurance because they were worried about their health or possibly were even ill. Thus, the charts which I and millions of others regarded so long as the gospel truth were not at all based on the everyday citizen existing in the real world.

These charts did not take into consideration the different builds and bodily differences of normal people. Athletes, for example, in prime physical condition, could be adjudged too heavy if height-weight figures for the so-called normal man were used against them.

OLD CHART

DESIRABLE WEIGHTS BASED ON INSURANCE COMPANY STATISTICS FOR WOMEN AGES 25 AND OVER:

HEIGHT		Small Frame	Medium Frame	Large Frame
4	10	100	107	117
4	11	103	110	120
5	0	106	113	123
5	1	109	116	126
5	2	112	120	130
5	3	115	124	134
5	4	119	128	138
5	5	123	132	142
5	6	127	136	146
5	7	131	140	150
5	8	135	144	154
5	9	139	148	159
5	10	143	152	164
5	11	147	157	169

NEW CHART

BASED ON 20% INCREASE OVER THE FIGURES SHOWN ON CURRENT CHARTS FOR WOMEN AGES 25 AND OVER:

HEIGHT		Small Frame	Medium Frame	Large Frame
4	10	110-118	115-128	125-143
4	11	113-121	118-132	127-146
5	0	115-125	121-136	131-150
5	1	119-128	125-139	134-154
5	2	122-132	128-143	138-157
5	3	126-136	132-146	142-161
5	4	130-139	136-151	145-166
5	5	133-143	139-156	150-170
5	6	137-148	144-162	155-175
5	7	142-152	149-167	160-180
5	8	146-157	154-172	164-185
5	9	151-162	158-176	169-190
5	10	156-168	163-181	174-196
5	11	161-173	168-186	179-202

Weight in Pounds According to Frame (In Indoor Clothing)
(For girls between 18 and 25, subtract one pound
for each year under 26.)

I would laugh at the ridiculousness of chasing down numbers on those charts all my early years if it weren't for the awful burden needlessly imposed upon me and millions of others. It's as if a cruel, sadistic joke were played on us all. We were sold a bill of goods, and not one of us had the common sense to challenge the wisdom of insurance megacorporations. Instead of heeding the bathroom scale, we should have stepped onto a *value* scale and relied on a look in the mirror regardless of age, size and weight.

We have the power to call a halt to this madness. We must learn to say no to those people and industries that manipulate us and our children. Why not?—we've learned damn well how to say "No" to ourselves all these years because that's all we figured we deserved—negative reinforcement. We tacitly agreed with the perpetrators of crimes against us. It's time to stop this evil trend—time to say "No" to hatred and "No" to a 'fashionable' waistline—time to say "Yes" to life and to enjoy a happy existence with our kids. All this worry about weight is like a traffic jam holding us up from getting where we ought to be.

OBESE IS AS OBESE DOESN'T

It has taken me over 40 years to drop out as a footsoldier in the war against fat. Right now I do not consider myself obese at 200 lbs., no matter what *any* chart might say. To me, obese has with it the limitation of a loss of function. An obese person is someone with a handicap, restricted from performing tasks, just as a blind person or an amputee. As long as I live my life with zest, with verve, and with good health, I am *not* obese.

People on the telephone occasionally ask me how much I weigh. I tell them 200 lbs. In their mind's eye, these people see me as a woman who waddles, whose arms cannot touch in back, and who has to be helped out of chairs.

When I finally meet them in the flesh, many times they will blurt out, "Why, you're not so fat!" This annoys me. It's as if they're saying "You're not so black!" or "You're not so Jewish!" or "You're not so ugly!" What they are intimating is that I'm one of the "good" ones—one of that type who is acceptable. This statement rings in my ears as an insult, albeit a well-intended insult, an Archie Bunker-type slur.

We have certain inalienable rights as human beings. One of these rights is to walk the streets freely without fear of insult. We don't let people whose religious beliefs or political beliefs differ radically from ours malign us. Yet when it comes to weight, many of us clam up in the face of ridicule.

31

Why should those people whose shallow value system espouses thinness as the *only* way to be, push the rest of us around? Why should they make us unhappy? Who gave them that right?

The answer, sadly, is that *we* did. We gave them tacit permission to censure us. We have suffered in silence alone until *now*. It is time we *revoked* that permission from everyone and started dealing from a position of strength.

Nothing is wrong with being big, but we big women have been programmed since birth to think it's wrong. Are you going to chastize an Eleanor Roosevelt or a Golda Meir for having a chunky behind?

If we lived in Victorian times, our input from the outside world would be supportive. "Oh Carole!" the Victorians would have exclaimed. "You are built like a *real* woman. You are *so* beautiful."

In those days if someone would have come up to me and said "You're too fat!," I would have said: "Don't be ridiculous. I'm terrific!" My response would have been instantaneous because I would have felt my size was desired by society. I would have been the norm, while conversely, a thin girl was dealing from a position of weakness.

"You poor thin sickly girl!" we *real* women would have scoffed. "You'll never find yourself a man."

It is necessary to turn your thinking around 180 degrees and deal with society from a position of strength. It's not easy, but it can be done.

Myth:

FAT WOMEN SHOULD NEVER TUCK THEIR BLOUSES IN OR WEAR BELTS BECAUSE THAT MAKES THEM LOOK FATTER.

False.

Tucking in your
blouse or wearing
a belt does not
make you look
fatter or thinner.
It just makes you
look neater!

2 | HANGING UP OUR HANGUPS

Is a skinny woman really more valuable to society than a fat woman? In *her* eyes, she's not. Why? Because thin people face the same pressures about weight that heavier people face. Many women put the same stress on themselves for going five pounds over 120, as those of us who've gone more than 50 lbs. over.

The problem is that *all* women are taught from girlhood to despise their bodies. Conjure up the prettiest female you know, someone with the most knockout figure that you can imagine, and ask her if she likes her body the way it is now. Without a doubt, she'll find something about her appearance to criticize. Perhaps she'll say her chest is too big (or too small), her hips too wide, or her thighs too flabby, or whatever. "I *really* must lose three pounds," she'll say, and never doubt that she is sincere. Women are pressured into running after some unattainable ideal of how we should look to ourselves and others. If American society put equal pressure on us for something intrinsically valuable such as painting, musical talent or other creative tasks, this country would be a society of artists.

There is nothing wrong with pursuing a goal for self-improvement. The key word here is *goal*, which implies choice, not a neurotic frenzied push toward impossible dreams of thinness. Moreover, such a mania is particularly hard on large-size women whose bodies were intended by Nature to be more full and rounded than the Hollywood version of a feminine shape. To strive toward attaining a

37

certain shape of body, no matter what the price, no matter what the stress, no matter what the effort, strikes me as distinctly unhealthy. What's so awful about being built for comfort—not for speed?

A FOOLISH, NEVER ENDING BATTLE

What about those very few "fortunates" who through starvation, duress and sheer endurance achieve fashion magazine bodies that are 5'8" and say, 98 lbs. Do you think even *they* are satisfied? Just ask any sex therapist who has his or her clients stand in front of a mirror to say something good about their bodies. Instead of picking out a nice nose, or eyes, or hips and breasts, or shape, or whatever, even these people will inevitably despise one body feature or another.

Society's values change with the season, and some seasons will exclude *any* woman's best features. Depending upon what's "in" at the moment, your hair is either too straight or too curly, too thick or too fine, too oily or too dry. After you solve the "problem," the cosmetic industry, diet industry and fashion industry have contrived for that season, there is always a new problem to make you unhappy. Fashion's newest death's head is, of course, cellulite.

AND MADISON AVENUE SAID, "LET THERE BE CELLULITE"

Cellulite doesn't even *exist* in medical terms. Essentially the term means that your skin (on your thighs, for example) puckers up because of how fat you are. But when I say "fat," I don't mean that just I, at 200 lbs., have to worry about cellulite. The woman who is three or four pounds over her ideal weight is the one who most dreads this manufactured source of emotional distress. Sometimes I wonder why *all* women aren't totally whacked out before they reach the age of 30.

Do you see the futility of this relentless pursuit toward changing, transient ideals of beauty? Do you see how frustrating it is to put all one's waking moments and energy into achieving physical successes which are turned into instant failures because some cupcake in Paris or on Seventh Avenue suddenly decides to alter "the" look? If you do, you're well on your way to achieving a position of strength. Once you concede that *no* one at *any* time is ever perfect, you're never going to punish yourself again because you aren't some stranger's ideal woman.

While you're at it, why not let this common sense approach to living help you overcome other areas in your life where "they" control your thinking?

LIVE FOR YOURSELF

Stop putting yourself in a little box and begin to feel free. Dare to be yourself. I get a lot of letters at BBW Magazine from readers who say they've always tried to be what others wanted them to be. Maybe it was the "best" daughter, or the "perfect" mate, or a "terrific" sport—whatever! That kind of thinking creates a person who wants to have just the right shape too.

Think of someone you know whose personal life is miserable even as she runs herself ragged trying to make those around her happy. Like a dog awaiting his master's pat on the head, these people wait (often in vain!) for some authority figure to say, "I'm so proud of you!" How much happier such a person (you, perhaps?) would be, pleasing herself. And just as no one can do the "right" thing at all times, so too there isn't a "right" shape or a "right" weight unless it's right for you.

CELLULOSE SILLINESS

Years of faithful moviegoing have made us programmed to feel that if someone has a handsome appearance, they must be intelligent too. The lone exception is the stereotyped dumb blonde, and that is equally false as an assumption.

Psychologists in a well known experiment gave pictures of incoming students to college professors, and the latter were required to rate how they thought students would do in class solely on the basis of appearance.

Overwhelmingly, the better-looking students were rated likely to be more intelligent and successful in the classroom. The instructors were also more likely to give a "break" to better-looking students on grades tottering between a "B" and "A", or "C" and "B."

The rest of us are no different. If you see a handsome fellow, you think he couldn't possibly be a burglar or a murderer or a rapist. Of course, this is far from true. Not all criminals and perverts are ugly.

Movies have rigorously enforced the stereotype when it comes to fat women by portraying them as maids, someone else's mother, or sex-starved comic types, always trying to lure the lodger to their room. Fat men have been stereotyped as mama's boys, child molesters, Fatty Arbuckle-type, pratfall comedians and homosexuals.

Recently in the film *Fatso* with Dom DeLuise, the hero waltzed off, not with another comedian or a fat girl but with the ingenue. This is the first time to my knowledge that the fat man won the pretty girl. No film yet has dared to pair a fat heroine with a gorgeous guy in any serious way.

BREAKING THE MOLD

We real life characters must realize that the movies rely totally upon stereotypes. These stereotypes get their validity from our endorsement of them. If we are to gain inner peace with ourselves, we must break the stereotypes, knowing that many fat people do *indeed* get the mate of their dreams. In life or in love, entering into anything with a defeated manner only leads to inevitable defeat.

We must not allow anyone to give us a reason for disliking our bodies. In reality, those qualities good and bad that we attribute to our weight are really our own inherent qualities for which we do not want to take responsibility. (I'm ugly because I'm fat, or conversely, I'm wonderful because I've become thin.)

DON'T WAIT FOR YOUR SHAPE TO COME IN

Whatever your shape, it is *yours* temporarily or permanently. Hating your shape, whether it is fat or thin, only lowers your estimation of yourself as a total person. If you're so ashamed of your body that you hide yourself in dresses that look like Omar's tents, your hatred is twice-cursed since you hate your clothes as well as yourself. The original crime is doubled. When you dare to tuck in your blouse instead of letting it bag, you don't look any larger. You're merely defining the boundaries of your body. You no longer feel like the shapeless blob who covered the earth.

Start seeing yourself for what you really are: a unique person with fine qualities, many still untapped perhaps, because you've allowed weight to hold you back. Why judge yourself so harshly? While it is true people see your weight first upon an introduction, it is also true that the people worth valuing quickly begin to look for those qualities that make up the *real* you. No sensible human being will dismiss you just because you are large, but they *will* do so if they see you as an insecure, self-loathing individual. Judge yourself by the qualities beyond the superficial you. Let the airheads criticize your fat if they want; you don't really need them around anyway.

Why do so many individuals and groups exhort us to be thin? No one ever formed a group to eliminate tall people, although there are groups of tall people who use that bond in common to hang around together. What's more, no fresh boor is likely to stroll up to a complete stranger and ask, "How come you're so tall?" People accept tallness.

Fat, however, is another matter. Through starvation and self-denial we can alter the state of our bodies—even if we have bone structure much more suited to holding more than the average person's poundage. There is *only* so much that can be done. A girl whose hips are quite large in proportion to her upper torso is not going to even things out when she diets. She is always going to have those large bones in her behind. What else can she do? —bang them with a rolling pin or pay a masseur to pound her into thinness twelve hours a day? Even if she does shrink her behind, it will still be out of proportion to the rest of her frame.

YOU'RE NOT THE ONLY ONE

A decade ago I reached the lowest point of my life: A size 20 dress no longer fit me. Never before or since have I hated myself so much. I've seen movies where jail doors slam in front of a prisoner, and that same feeling of aloneness overcame me when I found myself locked inside a (brace yourself!) *Women's Size 20.* Words cannot convey the horror I felt, and yet—even then—I was on a diet.

I went shopping like a criminal on the prowl, entering the dreaded large-size section and casing the area several times before plunging toward the racks. When finally I began flipping through the hangers, I found the clothes abominably ugly. They were a size six buyer's vision of what a size 20+ deserves to look like to atone for the sin of becoming fat.

To compound my problems, my back, which had troubled me before, now began to cause me excruciating pain. Prior to this time I had been hospitalized with back trouble several times, but I had always been able to function. Now, however, the discs, which previously had caused much discomfort, suddenly exploded. I went into spasms of agony, which literally never stopped for nine months. I had to have back surgery.

I took all the painkillers; I saw all the doctors; I read everything I could find on back trouble. Always the grim possibility that I might

41

live my life in a wheelchair hung over my head.

The operation, thank God, was a complete success. But would you believe that I put myself on a diet the day that I came out of intensive care? Once again I began to strive toward that 120 lb. plateau.

However, the day I was to be discharged, quite by accident I obtained a copy of the surgeon's log of the operation, the report he sends the insurance company. What I read there shocked me and made me re-examine my life as nothing had ever done before. While I was inert on the operating table, my heart had stopped pumping and had overreacted to a muscle relaxer.

When I finally stepped outside the hospital, I felt like I had been given a second shot at life. It was a beautiful afternoon in February. The colors of the sky, grass, trees, buildings and cars came pounding in on me. When I saw my husband's face as I climbed into the car, I said, "Son-of-a-gun, I'm *supposed* to be here!"

NO LONGER DO OR DIET

From that moment on, dieting became a stupid and meaningless thing to do when placed in the context of what human life is worth. I was never able to stay faithfully on a diet again. My diets were of shorter and shorter duration, until finally I achieved a position of strength. As a result of that operation, after I had in fact died for several seconds, I was able to see things from a fresh perspective. I began to count my blessings instead of calories.

LOOK BEFORE YOU BELIEVE

You also can achieve the same position of strength, and you don't have to suffer physical torment to do so. How do you get there? By backing off from the things you have always held to be true. Examine those beliefs displaying the same skepticism that any scientist holds for an unproved premise—the same skepticism, for that matter, with which you are hopefully reading these words. Think before accepting what you are told.

THE TRUTH WILL MAKE YOU FREE

I propose that we free ourselves from making a hell out of life on earth. We large people must lose the attitude that we deserve abuse from others. Many of us believe there must be some flaw in our characters if we cannot take off pounds "like everyone else." One reason that many of us *do* have hangups and insecurities is because others show us contempt. Such people deserve to be treated in like fashion or to be ignored. They are trying to melt us down to fit an anonymous mold, and I resent their attempts to turn us all into raving maniacs because our bodies don't fit the image cast by *Cosmopolitan* Magazine. Wasn't it God who created us in his image—not Helen Gurley Brown?

Myth:

WOMEN ALWAYS LOOK BETTER IN THOSE ADS FOR DIET PRODUCTS **AFTER** INSTEAD OF **BEFORE**.

False.

*Everyone knows that makeover photos make a woman look awful in those **before** shots. Two can play that same game, as these photos prove. P.S. In case you're interested: The 'before' picture is me at age 33 and 127 lbs. — The 'after' is age 46 and 200 lbs.*

3 | Part I—THOUGHT FOR FOOD

Dieting is something we all take too seriously in this day and age. A magazine article in the Washingtonian says that the publication of a new diet book is like sending millions of people after a latter-day Holy Grail. If a book ever outsells the Bible, you know it will be some "sure-cure" diet. But after all, dieting isn't a religion.

Dieting must be your personal decision. If you want to diet—terrific. If you want to *wait* until you want to diet—terrific. If you never want to diet again—terrific. It's your decision.

It took me nearly 40 years to come to grips with the issue of dieting. I may diet again. That's my right. But never again will I drop down to some arbitrarily arrived-at weight for my size and bone structure. Never again will I starve myself down to 120 lbs.

NO APOLOGIES

One of the nicest days I've spent recently was with five models who went with me to San Diego for a TV show. Since we had to be at the studio at 7 a.m. and had endured a two-hour drive from Los Angeles, none of us had breakfasted before the show. By the time we left the studio it was nearly 11 a.m., and all of us were ready to devour an elephant.

We marched *en masse* into a nearby coffee shop, making heads turn. You couldn't miss six, big, well-groomed, smartly-dressed, hungry-as-hell BBWs. We sat down at a round table and started ordering without benefit of a second glance at the menus.

We were *hun-gerrry!* Each girl snapped off her order like a Marine Corps drill instructor. Boom! Boom! Boom! Eggs, hash browns, juice, toast, side orders of pancakes and huge steaming pots of coffee.

Not one person sniveled into her menu. There wasn't a single, "Oh, I really shouldn't" or even an "I'm so naughty!" or "There goes my diet!"—the balderdash one usually hears when dining out with other females. These women sat down and ate their food like they enjoyed it, which of course they did. The laughter flowed, the conversation never stopped, and it was one of the most enjoyable meals in my memory. I picked up that tab gladly and thought every dime of it was well-spent. We sang all the way home.

STOW THE DIET TALK

I get letters from men all the time who say how much they abhor escorting their women out to a gorgeous restaurant like Regine's in NY, springing for an enormous tab, and then being forced to listen the entire evening to dieting tales of woe. It is *boring* for anyone but another dieter to endure a harangue about what can and can't be put inside one's belly.

If you're on a diet—fine and dandy. Scan the menu with care and order something compatible with that diet. Don't burden your companion with the sob story of how *you* are sacrificing when you order a $40 meal at *his* expense.

Doesn't it make more sense while ordering the broiled red snapper (No butter, please!), to tell your companion how you simply adore the taste of fresh fish—very dry? If you're going to make *his* dinner an exercise in sacrifice, don't accept an invitation to eat. Accompany him to a movie instead—if you can keep your mouth shut about diet talk when he offers you some of his buttered popcorn.

Think of the decision to diet as an extremely personal endeavor, one that you choose not to discuss with anyone else. At a cocktail party, you don't encourage people to ask how much you paid for your house, how often you have sex each week, or whether your children are squandering their lunch money in an opium den. I mean, these are all extremely personal affairs.

Everyone in polite society is aware of certain lines you don't cross. Doesn't it seem a bit pushy of someone to approach a large-size person and to ask what diet they are on? Isn't that a display of incredible gall and presumption to assume that another person must be so unhappy with his or her God-given body that the individual *must* be plotting how to do away with it?

I personally find it extremely disconcerting and in bad taste for anyone to monitor or censor another person's eating habits. Based solely on your size, some *im*perfect strangers think they have permission to chide you for what you put into your mouth—even if *their* plates contain exactly what *you* are eating.

There isn't a big person in the world who hasn't at one time or another been asked: "Do you really think you need that dessert?" I can't imagine how a *relative* could ask that, let alone a total stranger. I mean, could you in your wildest dreams imagine going up to these same people and asking whether they really need that expensive Porsche Targa, wetbar, or another long weekend in Majorca?

IS THIS FAIR?

Haven't there been times when you've skipped breakfast and lunch to dine at a gorgeous buffet—only to be intimidated by others in line to the point where you selected the smallest portions from the most unappealing offerings? And haven't you known many big women who, even when they were not on diets, were made so uncomfortable while lunching with dieters that they too ordered rabbit food? People assume that since you're big, you must be dieting. Is this fair? Why such outrage if a big woman orders a slice of cheesecake, or a big man buys an ice cream cone?

All I can figure is that the big man and the big woman are flaunting what society has drummed into most of us: Anything that tastes so good must be a sin. So it offends people when we have the nerve to enjoy what we eat. Maybe these folks feel resentment because they would like to enjoy the foods we are enjoying, but refrain for fear of losing the figures society says they must possess. For years and years whenever waiters came around to take dessert orders, I told them: "No thanks! Not for me." Until finally it hit me. Why *not* for me? Why for everyone else at the table but not for me? And why should I offer the expected apologies to the waiter and anyone within five tables away about how naughty I was being if I decided to have dessert?

I mean, even if I dined *alone* in a restaurant, I used to decline the Lobster Newburg. I was ashamed to ask for a gooey dish with cheese; I was afraid of what the waiter might think. Why didn't I realize how foolish I was being? Waiters don't give a carrot stick in hell what goes on a plate. It weighs the same and takes just as much effort whether you order a small chef's salad or Eggs Benedict. The chef certainly doesn't care either. Then why should we worry about ordering what we would get the greatest amount of pleasure from eating?

I've always said that I've come by my weight honestly. If there is blame to be laid for my size, let me place it squarely where it belongs: on my appetite.

It's a simple fact of life that I like the taste of food. Yet I am *not* a compulsive eater by any means, and I resent the belief that many people hold which is if you're fat, you must be compulsive.

PROFESSIONAL KNOW-IT-ALL

Recently, I met a hypnotist who is a very pragmatic man. He doesn't believe in regression to another lifetime, UFO's, or anything other than that which is provable by scientific evidence. The discussion came around to *BBW Magazine*, and he mentioned that he was very successful treating obesity with hypnosis. As a tall man, he told me his own weight was once 275 lbs., but now he was down to 195 lbs.

The conversation was quite interesting until he said something which set me off. "My problem," he said, "was that I was a compulsive eater."

"Do you feel that all fat people are compulsive eaters?"

"Most!" he nodded.

"Do you know the condition called 'anorexia nervosa'?"

"Yes, that's when someone literally starves to become thin."

"Right," I said. "Would you say that someone suffering from anorexia is a compulsive personality?"

"Of course."

"So most thin people are compulsive, right?"

"No, of course not."

"Of course not. But you said most fat people are compulsive."

The hypnotist's brand of *illogic* curls my straight hair. To me a compulsive eater is someone who does harmful things against Nature to her body. A very unhappy person might compulsively turn to food and get fat, but that person wasn't meant to be big. That's a thin person in a fat person's body, which is what the hypnotist and others accuse *all* of us as being.

When so-called experts generalize about fat people and call us *obsessive* or *compulsive*, it angers me. It's as unintellectual a judgment

50

as it is unfair. It's like saying that because you like sex every day you must be a nymphomaniac. Or, that all Italians are Mafia members. Or that all Jews are chicken soup addicts. Or that blondes have more fun (doing *what* I wonder!). While there may be a fat, Italian, blonde nymphomaniac of the Jewish persuasion who eats chicken soup while having lots of fun, this is certainly *not* the norm.

You've heard the saying, "Inside every fat person there's a thin person trying to get out." Not so. After all my years of dieting I discovered inside most fat people there's a fat person wishing the thin world would just leave him the hell alone.

Sometimes I think how nice it would be to go back to an Age of Innocence, that point where you are oblivious to what the "world" thinks about you. I recall as a little girl going to a store to pick up some cigars one time for my father, but by the time I arrived the name of the brand he wanted had slipped my mind. I looked up sadly at the store owner and admitted I'd forgotten, but after taking a closer look at me he handed over the correct cigars. "You must be Sam's daughter," he said after scrutinizing me.

What he was saying, in other words, was that I had to be my father's offspring because I was sturdily built the way he was. Being only six years old at the time, I took that as *such* a compliment. Look how the world knew I was my daddy's daughter. I look like him; I'm built like him. A few years later, when the realities of the world closed in on me, I would have died if some store owner said the same thing to me.

THE JOY OF VICTUALS

I still maintain that many, many fat people are far from compulsive about food. We love to eat. We experience great joy when we eat. We like everything about the act of eating: the taste, the aroma, the feel, the texture. I like to eat when I'm in the presence of good company, enjoying a spirited conversation in an elegant restaurant with lovely ambience. However, this is far from stealthily creeping up at all hours to raid the refrigerator! That's a whole different ballgame.

Food today has taken on an almost base connotation in certain circles. Rather than a source of life to be revered, it has become something despicable. Some put food into the same category as addictive substances such as alcohol and drugs. However, you don't get arrested for being fat, nor are you in danger of killing someone while driving under the influence of overweight. We get such contradictory messages about food that it is a wonder many of us don't wind up on a funny farm. Well, come to think of it, many of us do wind up on fat farms, however posh, which are only a step away from being institutionalized.

YOU GOT TO BE CAREFULLY TAUGHT TO HATE YOURSELF

We all start out in this life in its truest form. Every new mother feeds her baby of herself and rejoices over every ounce consumed, knowing that the child's chances for survival are increasing and that all its organs are receiving nourishment. The mother smiles and clicks her tongue at the wonderful fat thighs and wrists of her newborn offspring. I wonder if the fashion industry will take even this pleasure away from us now that Calvin Klein and Jordache jeans are offered for toddlers. Judging from the starkly cut garments they offer to us adults, I wonder if in our lifetime we'll live to see Metrecal-babies.

Part II—
CONFESSIONS OF
A DIET JUNKIE

People who are always on diets are forever inventing ways to beat those diets. That fact has helped Weight Watchers collect millions of dollars. Their function is to let members eat a lot of food and still lose weight.

Whenever I went on a diet, I'd always try to find a way to circumvent it. Like everyone else, I was a glutton for diets. Whenever a new one came out, I wanted in. The results, however, were always the same. I'd lose some poundage and promptly gain it back again.

Every time I went on a diet, in effect I told myself that there was something wrong with me as a person. In retrospect, perhaps I should have considered my dieting as a form of re-decoration. We don't have to hate a room to buy new furniture or to repaint our walls a different color. Why can't we be as kind to ourselves as we are to our living rooms? If you should decide to diet, you must still see yourself as a worthwhile person.

It's also wrong to work on the principle that something about food is inherently dangerous or undesirable. This belief is reinforced in magazine articles, health books and diet manuals. We come to regard food as evil temptation. We even call some foods "forbidden." We view these foods as the wicked equivalent of heroin and run to take our daily fixes of the dieter's methadone: cottage cheese.

Most people when dieting feel sanctimonious about self-denial. Contrary to the bright artwork on diet book jackets and magazine come-on ads, nothing takes off pounds painlessly. Dieting always hurts. The name of the game is deprivation. Unfortunately, many of us deprive ourselves of the food we want and may even need—only to stuff our bellies later with unwanted, often untasted food to fill that nagging urge. How many times have you forced yourself to endure a 12 calorie breakfast, only to gobble down, an hour later, a plateful of greasy-spoon eggs that taste like tire patches?

Self-control is not limited to our ability to deprive and deny ourselves. We have control when we grant ourselves permission to choose a life in which we enjoy food and feel good with our big, beautiful bodies.

Being thin does not mean never having to say you're sorry. Being thin does not mean that everything in your life will work out right— or indeed *has* to work out right. I never believed in the saying, "Good things come to those who wait." I believe even less that good things come to those who diet. After all, with better than 30 years of dieting behind me, the only thing that has stayed thin is my hair.

Another point that always has bothered me about dieting is that it's supposed to be a be-all and end-all cure for what ails us.

Recently, for example, I browsed through an issue of *Glamour* magazine. There was a typical before-and-after story about a girl who went from 209 lbs. to 135 lbs., and how this weight loss has affected her life. The story details how shy and unhappy she was at her top weight. They show you a picture of her "before," and of course there she is in a polyester pull-on pant and a maternity blouse, sans make-up or hairstyle. There are lots of photos of her exercising, and finally the girl is shown at 135 lbs. Her hair is now terrific (is that a hair lightener I detect?), and her makeup is perfect. She is flawlessly groomed. Her new clothes are adorable.

TRICK PHOTOGRAPHY

Nowhere is there the realization that the girl (whose name is Mary) felt terrible about herself because she *looked* terrible. The *reason* she looked terrible could just as easily have been due to her awful clothes and nonexistent grooming as it was to weight. I guarantee that Mary would have looked equally awful even at 135 lbs. clad in ugly clothes and without all the expertise that went into her hair and makeup. Caution! I didn't say she wouldn't look thin at 135 lbs.—she'd be thin all right—but it's possible that she would be fashionably thin and looking like hell.

The final paragraph of the magazine article is quite telling. "And what do Mary's friends think about her now?" we are asked with bated breath. "Mary's still Mary to us." I thought, "Oh, my Lord! This girl went through incredible tortures, and none of her friends can see any real changes." Mary is always going to be Mary. If Mary was a loner at 209 lbs., it wasn't necessarily because she was fat. More likely it was because she was shy. If she's starting to feel good about herself now, she could have felt good about herself then too. If only someone had taken the time to teach her about grooming and fashion. Perhaps she is now stuck in a position that may cost her more in effort and aggravation than it is worth.

Let's say that Mary does put the weight back on, as happens more often than not. Does this mean that Mary will forget everything she's been taught about clothes selection, grooming and beauty secrets? Will she be depressed and hate herself? The answer depends upon how healthy Mary has become mentally and emotionally.

All of us eventually learn that if you think it is hard to diet, it is equally hard *not* to diet. You are so programmed to begin each Monday with a fresh regimen of self-deprivation that you never really get out of the habit of mentally believing that all things pleasurable are illegal, immoral or fattening.

If you just cannot bear the thought of not being on some sort of diet, perhaps instead of going on another faddish weight loss program, you might undertake a "Love Yourself Diet."

CHOOSE ANY OR ALL OF THE FOLLOWING:

Morning: Reach over your right shoulder and give yourself six reassuring pats on the back

Have a loved one (if available) give you a suitable peck on the lips, cheek or forehead.

Take your left hand in your right and give yourself a firm and comforting handshake.

Afternoon: Take a walk outside and flash someone a cheery, "Hello." If it's returned, follow up with a friendly grin.

Several small portions of contentment for doing three nice things for someone else.

For dessert, practice a comforting wink which says, "Everything is OK" and bestow it on someone you like.

Evening: A full course meal consisting of a bearhug from a loved one or a loving letter which you send someone far removed from your presence. Seconds and thirds are permitted.

Once you decide to reject society's need for eternal dieting, a funny thing occurs. You find that you really don't own the mouth that will destroy the world's food supply. You only want a slice of banana coconut pie once in a while, not before and after dessert or every waking moment of the day as you had feared. In some cases, when you give up dieting and eat what you want, your weight actually goes down. Food isn't always on your mind as it was when you were dieting. You aren't as despicable as you thought.

At the very worst your weight will stabilize at some comfortable point. You then may join that elite group that you've spent your life envying—those people who eat anything and everything they want without ever adding a pound. Over a 24-hour period they have an urge for a salad or a piece of broiled chicken to balance the triple scoop ice cream and triple decker soda we saw them sip. Their appetites have a chance to balance out. We dieters, on the other hand, never learned how to balance our desires because we were too busy stuffing ourselves with every allowable item on our diets, and then guiltily binging hours later to make up to ourselves for the fact we are still starving.

Think about it. After years of longing for a big breakfast, what's going to happen when you finally indulge? Do you *really* think you'll crack open seven eggs and two packages of bacon? Probably not. You'll make three eggs—maybe!—and an extra piece of bacon or two. Nor will you fry your eggs in a pound of butter. You'll use only enough to help you get over the memory of years spent devouring those awful soft-boiled or poached eggs. (And *dry* toast—Ugh, Ugh, Ugh!). What I'm getting at is that most of us big people simply want a regular 'real person' breakfast topped off with juice and coffee. Is that such a terrible thing?

To break the diet habit you need a phrase to believe in, and that phrase is: "I'm worth it." It's not going to be easy to turn your life and guilt around when you stop your constant dieting. My two biggest shocks after I quit the eternal diet habit were that I often didn't care for dessert and that I actually *liked* the taste of cottage cheese. I also got out of that awful habit of awarding myself Brownie points in character and willpower whenever I ran into a person fatter than I.

Part III—
DIETS I HAVE
KNOWN AND LOST

When I think of how many diets I tried over the years, I shudder. No matter what era in my life, I can always remember what I was doing by recalling which diet I was following then. Here are a few of the more memorable reduction plans I've tried.

CALORIE COUNTING: 1947-1953

As a teenager, I became an unnoted authority on calorie counts. I could have spouted off the calorie total of every food from aardvark innards to zoo nuts. Other adolescents memorized historical dates or batting averages or Lana Turner's husbands' names. I studied a calorie counting book put out by a weightlifter named Joe Bonomo. If you asked for the calorie total in cabbage, I could have given it to you right off.

Others I've talked to who were big as children tell me that they did the same thing. That's why you'll never find a calorie chart or a diet discovery in *BBW Magazine*. I figure that since most of my readers are already experts on dieting, there is nothing new to tell them. Now they can tell you not only calorie totals, but carbohydrate content as well.

MAYO DIET: 1954

Whenever I hear the words "Mayo Clinic," I am in danger of gagging. For me, the Mayo Clinic is the Mayo Diet, which nearly turned me into an egg even as I invariably took off seven or eight pounds on it.

Back then doctors all swore that eggs were a healthy, nutritious food. Years afterwards they changed their minds and began berating us for consuming so much cholesterol.

Often I wonder how many successful Mayo dieters wound up clutching themselves like Fred Sanford as victims of "The Big One," or turned out to be the most fashionably skinny people in the intensive care ward.

METRECAL: 1958

Metrecal! That was the revolutionary concept that was really going to work for all of us. Metrecal powder came out in the late Fifties. We convinced ourselves that because it was *chocolate*-flavored, it really tasted wonderful.

In the end, Metrecal, like any other panacea for losing weight, turned out to be just one more carrot dangled in front of the fat people of America. It was doomed to failure from the start. Can you actually imagine any living person going through an entire lifetime existing only on Metrecal? How good can you make a bunch of chemicals taste, anyway? You can fool yourself into thinking you're guzzling a chocolate drink for only so long. Even if it *was* a chocolate drink, can you imagine anyone passing 21 of these a week through the old system?

DRINKING MAN'S DIET: 1963

A real hardcore gambler dies and goes to hell. When he wakes up he finds himself in a plush suite in a Las Vegas hotel. In this suite are baccarat and crap tables, gorgeous women and bartenders serving drinks. "This is hell?" he thinks. "This is hell?" He throws a couple of dollars on the crap table and rolls 40 'seven's' in a row. He goes to the slot machines and wins every time. This goes on for a day until the fellow is absolutely bored. He realizes that he is *always* going to win. For a gambler, there is no torture worse than boredom.

This story best illustrates the Drinking Man's Diet. It gave you permission to eat all the things you've always been told that you must never have on a diet. Oh joy! Oh heaven!

The Drinking Man's Diet says, "You want scrambled eggs fried in butter? Go, man, go! And throw on the bacon if you'd like. You want cheese, too? Why not?"

Naturally I was skeptical and immediately put the Drinking Man's Diet to the test. *Ordinarily*, I'd have a one egg breakfast with two slices of bacon. All right, I'll have three egg omelettes loaded up with lots of butter—a pound of bacon on the side—and lots of gooey, cheesy things on the inside. And you know, I lost weight, I really did.

Unfortunately, on that diet you are not allowed to eat fruit or vegetables. So after two weeks I had visions of the back of my throat as a large dam with a flood tide of orange juice passing through. I'd have robbed a Safeway for a piece of fruit or vegetable. I soon reached the desperation point that you always reach when you're denied something after which you hunger.

WEIGHT WATCHERS 1969

For many of us WWII does not mean World War II. It means the second time we were on Weight Watchers. I don't know if they still do it, but back in 1969 when I went to Weight Watchers, they gave me a pin for reaching my goal and a diamond for each additional ten pounds. If anybody wants a Weight Watchers pin with one diamond in it, I've got one for you. I'm the kind of person that when I go on a diet, I never cheat. If I break it, I break it, but never cheat. For three months I was an absolute disciple, and I lost 30 lbs. I went in at 157 lbs., and I came out at 127 lbs.

I remember that I was like a mad scientist. I had my little scale that I never left at home because you had to measure everything before you ate it, and I weighed everything scrupulously. My life was a series of one meeting after the next, hearing about new ways to outwit your body by ingesting 19,000 heads of lettuce. I got up in the morning thinking of bizarre but legal ways to make my allotted egg—and I can't even cook for God's sake!

The real problem is—when W.W. tells you—and you agree—that bean sprouts with tomato sauce tastes just like spaghetti, you no longer need Weight Watchers, you need a good shrink!

THE STILLMAN DIET: 1973

Oh Stillman, my Stillman, was the diet that kept the plumbers of America in business for years. The Stillman diet, you see, was also known as "The Water Diet." Everyone used to run around all day guzzing huge 12 ounce containers of water. You'd pass someone in a hall, and he'd be gulping down a glass and moaning: "Oh my God! I only had six glasses of water today, and I need two more." Dr. Stillman, you see, had mandated that all those who tried his diet drink eight to ten glasses of water a day. I mean think of all those poor kidneys bloating up in utter exhaustion when suddenly a heart or lung or something shouts out: "Watch it, baby! Six more ounces coming atcha!"

THE LIQUID PROTEIN DIET: 1975

Certain foods such as fruits and vegetables have a lot of carbohydrates which the body needs, or else the body goes into a form of insulin shock (ketosis). The object of the liquid protein diet was to get a slight ketosis by avoiding carbohydrates. It was a favorite of many doctors.

People were required to guzzle pre-digested liquid protein. Liquid protein, without a doubt, is the vilest tasting substance that ever passed through my lips. The object of the diet was to fast. You supposedly got all your nutrients, but you never had anything to eat—only this indescribably foul-tasting formula. You had to fortify the diet with potassium or else as you lost weight there was a slight complication. You died.

Many people who bought the stuff in drugstores without a prescription instead of getting it from their doctors didn't bother to read the instructions. They succumbed because the human body simply *must* have potassium.

Even now, when I think back to liquid protein, I find my lips curling in self-defense. Whenever you took a stiff belt it made you feel *so* sanctimonious. You always said to yourself: "I am a wonderful person because I can swallow this gunk so that I can lose weight. What a strong will I possess. What a saint I am."

In other words, another unfortunate side effect of the liquid protein diet was that you began acting like a jerk.

DIETS ARE LIKE TRAINS

Mercifully, I got off the diet go-round before the Scarsdale or Beverly Hills or the Bronx or the Cambridge diets. But diets are like trains—if you miss one, you can be sure another will be along in a very short time.

4 | SEX AND THE BBW

"Is it different making love to a large-size woman?" Tom Snyder asked me on his *Tomorrow Show*.

"How would I know?" I replied. "I've never made love to a large-size woman."

Although I was kidding, there is a lot of truth to this statement. I *don't* know what you do in your bedroom, nor do I feel overly inquisitive about your personal life either. What two people do in the privacy of their own bedroom is strictly their business. All I'll tell you is that under *our* covers, my husband and I leave the rest of the world behind.

NOT THE VOICE OF EXPERIENCE

What I say in this chapter comes from the experiences of my friends and readers, my limited experience, and just plain common sense. I can't draw from thousands of conquests like Xaviera Hollander. I do know, however, that many women are uncomfortable going to bed with new men because of fears about weight. This *is* something I can and will discuss in this chapter. But if you want 638 new positions you can do while dangling from a fire escape, you'll have to consult quite a different sort of book.

TO EACH HIS OWN

I get letters from men asking if I can introduce them to any girls over 400 lbs. Surprised? Who is to say that these fellows' needs are any more far out than the needs of men who go for model types whose skin is stretched cadaver-tight over their bones? Why is it all right for a man to date an extremely thin woman while taking a ribbing for dating an extremely fat woman?

Think about your own preferences and those of your friends. Some women like men with beards; others find facial hair a complete turn-off. Some big women only like thin men; others like men who match their size. Why should anyone apologize for what stirs the heart-a-fluttering?

When a man says, "I love your body and I want it," believe him. Don't say, "How could you when I weigh bla-bla pounds?" Do take "Yes!" for an answer.

Who says that a large-bodied woman won't turn a man on when she slips under the coverlet? Certainly not the boyfriends and husbands of large women.

Fat people are neither more nor less sexual than thin people. If we are in possession of a positive self-image, we are attractive to others and confident in our sexuality. Period.

I have to throw my hands up in consternation when a woman tells me her husband desires her 24 hours a day, but that she still feels herself totally undesirable until she loses weight. Has it ever occurred to her that it is her rounded, full-breasted feminine form that is turning her husband on in the first place?

GUILT WITHOUT SEX

Even more disturbing are those women who believe a man is actually some sort of *pervert* for showering them with attention. Dozens of readers have written that they were once promiscuous because they believed straight fornication was the only love they would ever receive. As a result, they took 'love' wherever they could find it, but felt horribly cheapened by these casual encounters.

These women all had in common a lack of respect for the men they were with. After all, went their reasoning, what were these guys doing with a fat woman in the first place? They knew a typical "date's" scheme. He was either very sick or very kinky. Since they had no love and respect for themselves, they didn't see how anyone else could love and respect them.

CHANGES IN ATTITUDE

Many of these women's attitudes toward themselves changed when they saw comely-looking big women staring back at them from the pages of *BBW Magazine*. Suddenly they said to themselves: "Hold on! I'm intelligent, fun to be with, a good dancer, cook, conversationalist—or whatever it is that attracts one person to another. Of course men will like me, they finally realize. I'm terrific!"

After these women start building up confidence, many find that men give them their first and second look, because they *are* heavy. You can go way back to Victorian times, or just to America's mid-Fifties, to find that full-bodied women were very much in demand. Thousands of men today display unabashed longing for amply formed women.

A Paris designer may wince at the sight of a voluptuous breast or rounded thigh, but many men say they hate to shake the sheets to find their women. They want lovers to look womanly, not like some models who seem but one organ short of looking like a little boy.

BIG *IS* OFTEN BETTER

When it comes to selling a sexier image, that Lincoln dealership of libidinous lingerie—Frederick's of Hollywood—makes a small fortune each year selling American women hip pads and inflatable bras. Women buy these "falsies" because their men prefer fuller figures. When it comes down to sex appeal, many women abandon their hipless Calvin Kleins for a look more in line with what men desire.

One of my favorite stories evolved during a fashion show in Dallas. I had just finished my spiel which included such remarks as "Eat your hearts out, Size Sixes!" and "Who can fill out a nightgown better than a big woman?" At the reception following the show I was approached by an extremely attractive large blonde woman. Beautifully coiffed and dressed, this woman spoke to me in a lovely Southern drawl. "I don't know why so many gals say they have a problem with may-yen," she cooed. "Mah husband is *very* happy and so is mah lover!" She was fantastic. I wanted to pack that woman along on my next tour just to have her repeat those two sentences over and over a-gay-yen.

Her point was simple but direct. She didn't know what all the fuss was about because she was getting hers and had been getting hers for a long, long time. She *feels* womanly. Therefore, she acts womanly and is treated like a woman in return. She believes that a man is getting the very best and owes her treatment which reflects that attitude as well. This is how all women must begin feeling whether size two or size 52, whether 16 years old or 80. Worry more whether your lover is worthy of *you* than you of your lover.

THE WORLD'S GREATEST LOVERS

Consider how many of the world's purported greatest lovers in real and literary life have been big women. Start with Cleopatra, then go to Chaucer's Wife of Bath, Flaubert's Madame Bovary, Lillian Russell, Sarah Bernhardt and Mae West. How many men do you know who would turn down a date with Miss Dolly Parton?

The great Italian actress, Anna Magnani, to name another notable beauty, was a big woman. She wasn't all that young either. Nor was she your typical silver screen beauty. Her fame was attributed to her animal-like, smoldering sexuality. She was cast in roles demanding a sexually attractive woman capable of inciting men to kill-ready lust.

Before you can convince a man that you are appealing, you must convince yourself that members of the opposite sex can and will go stark, raving bananas over you. Hey, not to brag (Oh, why not!!!), but I'm 200 lbs. and in my mid-40's, and every road trip I take puts me in a new hotel with propositions from handsome men (which I good-naturedly reject).

WHEN IN EUROPE

In fact, when I was in Italy, I found out in a hurry that Italian men go for big women. In Venice a fellow leaped off his bench and started singing "a capella" at the top of his lungs to honor *la bella signora*. It cracked my daughters up to have their mother treated like an international sex symbol.

On another location, I held up a long line of impatient customers at a roadside stop outside Florence while the restaurant ticket taker tried at length to proposition me on the spot. But my most memorable episode occurred in England when a handsome London gent approached and asked, "Where's your husband?" "In America," I answered. Whereupon he said, "Good!" and kissed me then and there on the street.

Now I am not so vain and foolish that I believe *every* man will want me, just as not every man will want you or Bo Derek either.

JUST NOT YOUR TYPE

Only in Madison Avenue commercials and ads are you assured of getting a lover if you're skinny. But then again, in those sales pitches you also get your man if you use the right toothpaste, perfume, shampoo, and whatever. It's all pure commercial nonsense, of course. Anyone who says that weight loss guarantees you a happy sex and love life is throwing out packaged phooey. Unhappiness in love is not the exclusive curse of large-size women. Just turn to this morning's Dear Abby column for proof to the contrary.

Please don't misconstrue this chapter to think that I believe the be-all and end-all of life is sex, or even the snaring of a man. Sex is only one part of a person's existence, and like anything else it varies on a one-to-ten scale with the individual. Someone may rate it as most important. Another may accord it a "who-needs-it?" rating. There is no standard-measure recipe for life. One size or shape or lifestyle is not right for all.

There is no earthly reason why a slender woman should be inherently sexier than a large woman. You must convince yourself that this is true. If you've spent a lifetime hating yourself and denying your sexuality, it will take time to change bad habits, but it is certainly the most important favor you can do yourself.

LOOK OUT FOR NUMBER ONE

First you must educate yourself. You cannot waste time foolishly trying to change the world. It has you outnumbered. The only person you have control over is yourself. Take control of yourself and your attitudes, and you *can* effect a change.

Now that doesn't mean that every living thing (male, female, animal or vegetable) is going to like you or return your affection in the same way. But then a "Size Two" does not get a standing ovation from every man she passes either.

People only react to you. *They* do not make you what you are. They cannot make you more or less than you are or can be; only *you* can do that. Remember, above all, sexiness is not how you look. Sexiness is how you feel and how you make your partner feel. If you don't feel sexy, why be surprised when no one else thinks you are either? People are merely confirming what you project.

All of us have sexual inhibitions of one sort or another. Even if your weight disappears overnight, many inhibitions won't.

69

LOVE DOESN'T COME BY THE OUNCE

When you smile at a person from the heart, is that a Fat Smile? When you share feelings with another, can those be called Fat Feelings? If you go after a would-be lover with everything you've got, do you have a Fat Chance? When someone—adult or child—throws his arms around you and says, "I love you!"—do you berate him for such Heavy Emotion?

Are you so concerned with being somewhere else or someone else that you lose touch with whatever enjoyment you could be extracting from the present moment? Watch people in a restaurant—many of them are swiveling around to check out the action around them, ignoring their companions. What a sad way to go through life. Someone who always wishes she were elsewhere isn't going to have a satisfying time anywhere.

These people crave the spotlight and are unconsciously plotting how to make their next moves. When the people with them are talking, their minds are on what *they* can say or do next.

No one is more attractive than someone who really listens to another person. That quality is irresistible. It transcends mere physical beauty.

HANDS DOWN WINNER

One way to find your real worth is to cease to concentrate on your body size as an index to your value and begin to look at yourself from a fresh new perspective. Take a close (No, closer!) look at your hands. Hands are a wonderful clue to character. They reveal whether their owner is hearty, a doer, a sedentary type or artistic. If you study them under a microscope they give you an inkling of the complexity and wonder of the human body. They also betray age. Who cannot differentiate between a young girl's hand and that of a woman in her 40's?

Nowhere do hands devalue you as a fat person. Anything thin hands can do, fat hands can do. Except for worry over dishwater hands, they are perhaps the only part of our bodies to escape a commercialized hard sell. Thus far, mercifully, we haven't had to check their weight on a chart or tag them with a designer label.

SEX ON YOUR MIND

When you make love, whom do you concentrate upon? If in the middle of passion your thoughts go to the editors of *Vogue,* your 103 lb. neighbor, or the instructress at Jack LaLanne's, something is wrong. With these folk on your mind, you have one hell of a crowded bedroom. Evict them. There's only room in bed for you and your partner.

Remeber, there is no such thing as a fat libido. Maybe a sick libido or an undernourished one, but fat plays no part whatsoever. When it comes to sexual lovemaking, we are down to our bare bones. It's not a case of what you *see* is what you get. It's what we *give* that helps determine what we get in return. In the arms of someone we love who returns our love, we are not young or old, beautiful or plain, fat or thin. We are instead part of a common instinct that extends back to the first dropped fig leaf.

Have you ever considered what an incredible undertaking sex is? On any given night people are coupling who have any number of differences between them. Weight and size are only two such differences. There's also, at times, vast differences in race, social status, financial position, age and ice cream flavor preference. One partner is more experienced. One is more adventurous. One is rebounding from a bad love affair or might have suffered sexual abuse. And so it goes.

Except on blessed occasions where bodies blend like amaretto and cream, you and your partner must put an effort into pleasing one another. This means that you must overcome any tendency to be inhibited because of weight. If you hold back because you're afraid he'll dislike your body in a certain position, you are cheating him and you out of pleasure.

LET YOURSELF GO

While sex is hardly a laugh-a-minute proposition, neither is it a teeth-grinding exercise. Nature made sex to release tension, not to increase it. Compare sex with the games you play for the love of them alone, the ones for which you never fake enthusiasm. When you're involved in something you feel genuinely good about, your own enjoyment and performance are naturally enhanced. Your most sparkling performances, your most brilliant moves, happen when you lighten up and forget about proving anything. The sheer joy of what you are doing carries you. Have a good time, laugh, and be merry in bed. Too often the witty fun self we display to woo someone is abandoned once loveplay commences.

When you are with someone you care for, you love them—warts, pimples, spare tire and all. When you look into a lover's eyes with feeling, you don't see eyes that are nearsighted. These are the eyes of someone you feel for with your soul, and his eyes are the gateway to his soul. I'm reminded of a favorite movie, *The Enchanted Cottage*, where a man disfigured in war and a painfully plain girl fall in love with each other. The rest of the world viewed them with revulsion, but when the lovers looked upon one another, they saw beauty.

Or consider the lovers in *Coming Home* played by Jane Fonda and Jon Voight. Was it hard to believe that a beautiful, sensitive woman could fall in love with a handsome, sympathetic man who had the misfortune to become a paraplegic in the Vietnam War? Only some-one preoccupied with mechanical sex could fail to identify with the feelings these two had for each other. Bodily imperfection might exist, but it is ignored because of the *value* of the other person.

FOR MARRIED WOMEN ONLY

I do lots of fashion shows every year in cities all over the country. Some women bring their husbands along to learn that their wives can be both big and beautiful. Often after a show these men will come up to shake hands and thank me. Fresh love glows in their eyes as they see how their wives can look once they've given themselves permission to be beautiful and to practice good grooming habits.

They loved their mates before, but they were inhibited because they thought society frowned upon loving a fat woman. By seeing all those bold, confident and incredibly sexy, large models parade before them, these men instantly found the courage to back their wives. Caught up in the excitement, many of the men want to go shopping with their wives to outfit them on the spot. It's very touching to see.

On the other hand, some men never will acquiesce to the idea that their wives are bigger than the Jones woman next door. These men are constantly on their spouses' backs about weight.

To my horror I've heard husbands belittle their wives publicly. One night after I appeared on a famous comedian's show, the star took the cast out to dinner where he proceeded to make scathing comments about his wife's size. By the evening's end his wife hadn't changed a bit, but this famous comic had forever shrunk in our sight.

To such women, I might say that there are likely problems with your marriage that have nothing to do with weight—problems that

73

will not disappear even if you're made unhappy enough to sweat off many, many pounds. A spouse might insist that fat is the reason he or she is turned off, but it rarely ever turns out to be the bottom line reason. It's just a visible place to hang a complaint.

Often these men are insecure about their own roles as males and are not strong enough to flaunt society's foolish values about weight. They are afraid to stand by their choice of woman. A man who is confident doesn't need a carbon copy woman to assure him acceptance and verification of his masculinity. He's got enough self-esteem to be his own man. Neither a woman, a flashy car, a gold necklace or a shirt open to the navel is going to make him any more or less of a man than he thinks he already is.

MAN OVERBOARD?

I feel very sad about men who turn traitor on their wives, but I really don't know what to say. Who the heck am I to tell some lady in Shaker Heights, Ohio, that she ought to leave a man she's been with for a decade—even if that ten years has been filled with near-unbearable mental cruelty over the issue of weight. The fact is that I *don't* have that right.

HELL ON EARTH

If we are shy, inhibited and indifferent, it makes no difference whether we weigh 200 lbs. or 100 lbs., says Marilyn A. Fithian, a coordinator of the Center for Marital and Sexual Studies in Long Beach, CA. Many of her patients who express fears about weight have only five to ten pounds to lose to be of Playboy bunny proportions. Yet they have such a poor self-concept, that these pounds might as well be 50 lbs. to 150 lbs. over their current weight.

What must it be like to be married to a man who pursues the issue of his wife's weight? If a relationship is based solely on physical appearance, what should his wife feel if *he* ever develops a spare tire, if *he* suddenly loses his hair, if *he* develops a few wrinkles, or if *he* is disfigured in an accident? Does she then return his nasty comments barb for barb? In that case, neither couple has to worry about dying. They are already experiencing hell in this life.

IS DISSOLUTION A SOLUTION?

Many divorced women—particularly those whose spouses have destroyed their self-confidence by tormenting them about weight—are horrified by the prospect of dating once again. When I was a kid, divorces were rare as hen's teeth. You endured because that was the only way. Today, divorce is the inevitable conclusion to about half of all marriages, and many fat women are thrust into the whole new ballgame of dating. Many are women my age who were brought up on yesterday's moral code. If they had swung as a kid, they would swing now as a divorcee—but such is not the case.

The first reaction of a divorced woman who is a size eight or larger is that she's got to lose weight. She sees herself in a competitive market for dates and thinks "What chance do I have if I'm fat?"

The pressure is doubly hard for women who are not only fat but pushing 40 or better. Many find that the available men their age are dating 18 to 25-year-olds. Such women do have a problem, but it's not their weight.

Perhaps because older men have the time and income that younger men do not, they can attract girls half their age who are drawn to money and success. The older man, adrift in a midlife crisis, turns to the younger woman as an anchor on youth.

The solutions for many women are to date much older or much younger men—or to compete by becoming as sexually desirable as possible through proper grooming, makeup, beauty secrets, and fashionable dressing. Women must also face up to the fact that they must take risks. They have to be willing to fall flat on their faces in order to succeed.

Many women who date regularly do so because they realize that some men are too shy to ask for dates. These women find partners by *actively* searching them out. Sure they get a few turndowns, but their chances for successful connections are dramatically better than the chances of those who mope at home.

Myth:

FAT WOMEN ARE ASEXUAL.

False.

How sexy would Jacqueline Bisset feel in a Mother Hubbard? We never lacked sexuality — only sexy lingerie. Ask our husbands and our lovers. Desirability doesn't stop at size 18.

5 | THE BBW AND SEX

Since each of us is blessedly different in our tastes, appetites and lifestyles—especially when it comes to an area as intimate and primary as sex—I felt that I would be cheating you if I speak only from my own experience which is peculiar to me, my age and my upbringing.

To aid me in showing you a variety of tastes, appetites and lifestyles I have called on some BBWs of diverse ages and interest to share their experiences and feelings with you. In particular, I thought you might be interested in the thoughts of other BBWs on their own bodies in relation to sexuality, love and romance.

This chapter is not to be misconstrued as a guide book or as a role model collection. The subject of the BBW and sex has never been discussed in an open and candid way before. There is nothing so enlightening as to realize you are not alone in your joys, triumphs, failures and fears. The point is that big women, like little women, have sex lives—some successfully and some not. Whether sex is good or bad has nothing to do with weight.

ALEXIS

Alexis is a 27-year-old graduate of the University of California at Irvine. Her professional interest is to pursue a career in opera. During the late Seventies, Alexis lived for two years in Madrid, studying classical singing and supporting herself as a teacher of English. She is single and fluctuates between a size 18 and 20 on a 5'10" frame.

I feel a tiny, little kernel of terror just before taking off my clothes during lovemaking. Of course, it's always clear to me that whoever is taking off my clothes already knows that I'm heavy, but I can never quite, quite believe that someone finds me totally attractive because I'm used to people making corrections on my body—until recently, at least. The man I'm seeing now is the first person whom I unreservedly believe finds me attractive just as I am.

Not that I think a big woman's softness is unattractive. I'm often told that it is very comfortable to make love to a round woman.

I refuse, however, to feel uncomfortable about my weight during lovemaking. I also refuse to feel self-conscious about walking around naked *after* making love. I used to worry about cellulite in the thighs, but now I figure that my lover already knows about my cellulite and accepts it. I like feeling sexy and walking around naked in front of someone I care for.

None of my lovers has ever referred to my weight by any unflattering nickname. One lover did call me "Pumpkin," but that had nothing to do with weight.

The issue of weight has come up more than once. There was one man who, toward the end of our relationship, sent me to Overeaters Anonymous. He insisted that I would be happier if I lost weight. I believed him at first, but I wound up breaking up with him because of his attitude toward my weight. The reason that I even listened to him at all is that I'm used to people telling me I should lose weight for my own good. My mom always tried to get me to lose. Most people think being thin is a standard for beauty. And since I've got such a pretty face—put that in quotes—everyone tells me it's a shame that I'm big.

However, the question of weight never came up with my boyfriends in Europe. Men reacted to me as an attractive woman, somebody exotic from the States.

I often associate rejection and weight—whether it's a romantic rejection or a professional one for a lost singing opportunity. If I don't get a part for which I audition, a voice tells me, "It's because I'm fat." That's a trick I played so I'd always have an excuse for failing. I didn't have to face the fact that perhaps I didn't sing as well as someone else,

or that a relationship failed for more important reasons than my weight.

If there's one thing I learned, it's that I don't think I *can* lose weight for anyone else. Otherwise, I would have done so a long time ago. Now that I've accepted my weight, I'm beginning to free myself from fears about rejection. I face failure now, and that's no picnic, but at least I'm honest with myself.

No longer do I believe people like my mother and those boyfriends who said I'd be happier if I lost weight. Within the past year I've been getting militant. I've said, "Enough of that!" It's been a pendulum swing in the other direction, but I'm getting to be happy with the weight that I want for *me!* Even if I do decide to diet again, I have no interest in being itsy-bitsy. I like the fact that I am a curvy person. I have large breasts, rounded hips and rounded thighs—I like them very much. I have no interest in being angular and bony.

I like large men. I've gone out with men smaller than I am, but I felt unbalanced—if you know what I mean. I dislike feeling larger than a man; I feel unfeminine. I especially like muscular men, but I also prefer a little flesh. Fortunately, many large, muscular men find large women especially attractive. I guess there are certain positions that are impaired by heavy buttocks, but other than that, I don't think large-size women have to restrict themselves from experiencing anything sexually.

I often have sex on a first date. It doesn't always work out though, so I don't know how good of an idea it is. Sometimes I think that it rushes a relationship. I sometimes feel that I got locked into certain patterns in a relationship by having sex too soon. It worked to my disadvantage, not the man's. When I have kids, I definitely plan to bring them up less sexually repressed than I was brought up.

ROSE

A published poet and associate editor of a national magazine, Rose left her husband of 24 years in 1980 to pursue a single life. Now in her mid 40's, she has eight children ranging in age from 11-23. She is proud of the success she's attained without having attended college. Her interests include music, sports and vacations in idyllic settings.

It's something else for a woman of 45 to go back to being single. I'm learning more about myself. My emotions just come rolling out. At this stage of my life without commitments, I am finally able to fulfill myself. Now there are no boundaries.

My views on marriage and sexuality have changed considerably since childhood. My background and beliefs taught me that when you get married you will be with only one person. I find that is a very unreal way to live, although I still think that it's the right and moral thing for married people. As a mature, single woman, I feel that I can have more than one relationship, and that is good.

Sure there are setbacks in my personal life; that's part of the everyday pattern of living. When I go into any kind of relationship that I'm sure I want, I proceed slowly. I'm acting on my emotions but they are in control. Before I make a commitment, I make sure that it's going to be good for me and that other person. I've been fortunate so far that it has.

I would advise someone newly divorced to hold back from sexual encounters until you are sure. I don't know if I could have handled a situation if a new man abused me because of my weight.

In the different groups I've joined after my divorce to help me decide who and where I am, the only thing I learned is that you don't really find *your* answers by observing someone else. You have to find things out for yourself. Don't be afraid anymore of whatever life has in store for you. Forget the past and look forward to the future.

A massive body change by dieting isn't going to make one bit of difference. You have to like what's inside you first. If you feel the divorce as a personal putdown, you must stop blaming yourself for being single all of a sudden.

A woman of 45 has much to offer in the way of an unscattered lifestyle. A woman at 45 who is complete and likes herself has more to offer than someone who is confused as to what life's about.

SUZETTE

Holder of a doctorate in psychology and president of an international consultant firm, Suzette says that she thrives on a free and easy single life. In her late 30's Suzette has bright red hair and calls herself "a queen-size lady" at size 22. She has been divorced for several years.

Weight played no factor in my divorce, and I don't think it plays a factor in any part of my life. Never in my life has there been a single instance when weight has made a critical difference. I don't criticize anyone else for idiosyncrasies whether it's gum chewing or cigar smoking, and therefore I do not permit people to suggest that my character traits are objectionable to them.

I feel *very* self-confident because I believe that to get a good performance in life, you need to make a good adjustment to yourself as to who you are, what you believe in and what you can handle. You can progressively handle more each day.

To handle various relationships, I think each woman has to know about *trick bags*. It's something you get yourself into where you're damned if you do or don't. For instance, a man might say: "I can't take you out because I don't like the way you look!" but, he might really be saying that he can't take you out because he doesn't have any money. You must not permit him to put pressure on you.

By the same token, a woman must also know what *trick bags* are her own. If we are promiscuous, and we sleep with a man who turns out to be a bad lover, we are going to be ashamed in the morning because we've wanted something that we haven't gotten. If it turns out that he's married, and we didn't ask him, and we have a brief fling with him, then we're in his trick bag if we're guilty or unhappy. We have to determine the price of the piper before we do anything instead of being a "Why not?" woman. Some men will say, "Why not? Let's just do it." This is fine if that's all you want. There's nothing wrong with treating a man like a sexual object, but know the value of this decision if you are going to feel guilty. Are you going to worry about getting pregnant? Are you going to worry that you're going to fall in love? Know the price ahead of time and quiz a man.

All it takes is 15 minutes to determine one way or the other what you will eventually do with a person if the situation arises. I've never found that I've been too bad of a judge. If I realize that I really want to sleep with a man physically, it wouldn't make any difference if he were married—nor would it make any difference if I never saw him again. This encounter might be something that you might want to do in a hotel in a strange city, but it might not be something you want to do in your hometown or the town in which your parents live.

As far as morality is concerned, I think the definition of promiscuity is anything that doesn't pay any dividends. I think a woman can be promiscuous with her own husband if it doesn't pay any dividends in the sense that she loves him, and he doesn't return her love and affection but gives it to other women. Anything that hurts you—where the piper's price is too high—is promiscuous as far as I'm concerned. What is right for younger women who sleep with a dozen or more men in a year may not be promiscuous, but for a woman who has only had sex with one man the last four or five years, even one occurrence could be promiscuous. I think it has to do with the future price you have to pay. I don't think it would necessarily be promiscuous when a delivery man comes to the door to make love when you've never seen him before and will never see him again. If the time is right and the situation is right, the goal we both achieve has value. You can have a love affair that doesn't have a beginning or end, but just is.

Most healthy men like women with 20 or 25 percent additional poundage. They do not like bony, skinny women. They are very fond of the mons veneris, breasts, buttocks, thighs and legs. I think those men who suspect a women with real breasts and real body substance, have something wrong with them.

However, what is important is hygiene. I think it is vital the way a woman smells. She must always take care of her teeth and her mouth. If you clean your teeth the minute you get up, it's the most important thing you can do for your sexual appetite.

Good seductive lingerie is very important, and I think you should always have a made bed. I don't think anything will turn off a man sooner than going into a room where the bed isn't made.

The song which says "You're nobody till somebody loves you" is absolute nonsense, because you can be somebody worth loving even if your nearest lover is 100 miles away. To be somebody worth loving you should cultivate the normal instincts of a lovable woman at all times.

TOY

For five years, Toy has interviewed hundreds of men on the subject of sex for publications owned by Larry Flynt and Hugh Hefner. Her views on what turns men on, as well as her own experiences growing up as a BBW, are quite enlightening.

I was 5'8" tall and considered 40 lbs. 'overweight' at 12 years old. I was taller than everybody else and to complicate things further, I was the only black, and a girl at that, in an exclusive Buffalo, NY prep school called Calasanctius. It was very, very traumatic growing up as a large person. I was always on pickle diets. That's all I ate. Pickles, I was told, had no calories.

I put myself on that diet. The problem I've found with all women is that they want to look like every other woman. *Women* set the standards of how they look—not men as you might think but women. I wanted to look like a model or an actress. I wanted to be a sexy, seductive model. My family, however, wasn't concerned at all with my weight. My father's side are all large people who come from slave stock. My two sisters and brother are larger than I am.

87

I went out with quite a lot of men when I went to Columbia-Barnard. I always thought that men wanted women to be what *they* wanted them to be. I rebelled against this attitude. I said, 'Take me or leave me; this is how I am.' I found out that I was fine and liked myself with or without weight. I had a tendency to go up and down the scale.

My own beliefs have changed quite a bit after interviewing so many men. I found that men have a real range in what they appreciate; you can't categorize them. Women think that men are attracted to a *Vogue* body, the super thin woman, but that's not true. Men like big boobs and a nice big behind and all sorts of things that women mentally don't find attractive. This goes all the way back into history whether you're talking about Venus de Milo or Rubens. It still holds today. Men like big women. They like to feel their softness.

In "skin" magazines we've run pictures of all sorts of models: big-breasted, small-breasted, long legs, shorter legs, every kind. From the letters I've received and the interviews I've done, there is a man to appreciate every type. It depends on the individual man and his own particular attraction. I find that American men, in particular, love breasts, big breasts. I would speculate that it is a comforting thing. Men are like boys. They want to be loved, they like to be cuddled. I think the typical American male wants a *real* woman: the strong loving type who works alongside her man and helps the country grow.

And I think a big woman is even more sexual than a thin woman. Let me qualify that. If a big woman is not overly hung up about her weight; she is more sexual. She can use her body, and men are very attracted to it. It's not the bigness; it's what's coming from within. If they're insecure, it's a turn off.

One of my best friends is very, very, very big, but she has more men around her than anyone I know. She's overweight as far as society's norm is concerned. Nevertheless, these men feel comfortable with her because she's comfortable with herself. It's not what you got. It's what you do with it.

On the other hand, there are women, both thin and fat, who are insecure. They feel they will never attract a man, and they won't. It's the *insecurity* that's a problem, not the weight.

It is also true that there are insecure men who will stay away from big women—despite their attraction—because they feel society wants them to go out with someone who fits into tight pants. It's their own egos which need building. They believe the commercials showing blondes with flowing hair and sunken cheekbones, open shirts down to the navel to show nothing underneath. They go for it because they are hypnotized, not admitting deep, deep down what really turns them on. When they grow up maybe they'll be able to admit that they like sinking into flesh, that they love the feel of breasts. It's much more sexual than to feel you're making love to one big elbow!

A woman has to be what is comfortable for her, despite any little 'so-called flaws' like weight, a belly, or whatever. No matter what size you are, that size is going to attract a man who is going to appreciate it.

It bothers me when relationships are based on superficial crap. Love each other based on what is inside; then weight won't matter.

GINNY

Ginny, 28, is 5'4" and 193 lbs. She has been happily married for six years to Len. "The nicest guy you'll ever meet." They live in a suburb of Dallas where they raise horses and care for their two daughters, Sally, age four, and Lexie, age 13 months.

I'm almost ashamed to admit it, but I was a virgin when I married Len. Don't get me wrong. I chose to be a virgin, and I've never regretted that decision for a moment.

I was always a 'big girl.' There has never been a time that I was thin. Yet, my parents, God bless them, never brought it to my attention in any way but that they were proud to have a daughter who looked like me. Especially my daddy. Maybe that's the key.

You see, because he always made me feel like a beautiful princess, it came natural for me to think of myself that way.

So later on when I started school, and the kids would tease me, I just felt that they obviously didn't know a good thing when they saw one. I went about my business and always found friends.

When I grew old enough to date, I looked forward to having a boyfriend, but I was so involved in school activities and so many courses and campaigns, that instead of meeting boys at the "meat markets" (school dances), I met them as people doing things they were enjoying and I was enjoying.

Many times friendship turned into boy/girlships. I liked being kissed and cuddled. I am a very affectionate person. No boy who ever dated me asked me to lose weight or made a comment about my weight one way or the other. I do remember more than one boy holding my hand or touching my arm and saying, "How soft and smooth you are." One time I asked a fellow, "Aren't all girls soft and smooth?" He just laughed and kissed me.

I met Len when I was 19. He was your typical Texas Cowboy. Strong, lean, muscled and all man. It was our love for horses that brought us together, but it was our great pleasure in each other's company that got us thinking seriously about a relationship.

Len asked me to marry him and to go to bed with him the same night. I said yes to the first and no to the second. And I kept saying no until the night of our wedding.

Finally, on my wedding night, there I was in a hotel room with the man I loved more than anything in the world. As I stepped out of the shower, I caught a glimpse of myself in the full-length mirror on the bathroom door. There I was. By all standards, an overly-abundant woman! Why did I feel so beautiful?

Was I nervous? Yes. But not about my body. I was nervous about being able to sense my brand new husband's needs in a situation in which I had no experience.

Not to worry. Len was experienced enough for both of us. I remember, that as I was touching his tight skin and feeling his muscled body and thinking to myself, "You married yourself a real man," Len turned to me and said, "You are the most complete woman I've ever known."

Myth:

FAT LADIES
DO NOT:
A) HAVE
   BOYFRIENDS
B) GET
   MARRIED
C) AND MOST
   CERTAINLY,
   DO **NOT** GET
   PREGNANT.

False.

Since 83% of women, size 16-52 are married and only 66.2% of women size 4-14 are married — we must be doing something right!

6 | DO MEN LIKE BBWs?

Sex and eating patterns are the most thoroughly ingrained of all personality traits. Food to our contemporaries is what sex was to the Victorians. The input of society to nineteenth century people was that sex was wrong and shameful—something to be done in darkest secrecy with extreme guilt arising later. The situation today is obviously the same for twentieth century people with regard to food. Society says we must repress our basic urge for nourishment and pleasure in nourishment.

Since food and sex are interrelated, we big women have heard over and over again that the penalty for Epicurean gratification is that no man can find us attractive and desirable. Not used to hearing the other side of the coin, we have come to believe this crock of nonsense.

Of course, some men do have a basic sexual attraction to thin women and we all know big women who prefer thin fellas—right? However, many men are knowingly or unknowingly cast into bondage to the establishment. Along with their foreign sportscar, designer clothes and other outward signs of "success," they believe there is only one type of woman with whom they may safely go out.

Richard Simmons, in his rather cruel best-seller, *Never Say Diet*, advises his readers to beware of "fatty chasers"—those who like big people. It never occurs to him that a good proportion of American men are "skinny chasers"—running after a feminine ideal that has been prepackaged and sold to specification.

95

But fortunately there *are* real men out there, and they are in America, too, not only in Europe. Men who are sufficiently secure with themselves to admit that they prefer dating or marrying a big woman. They know that life is too short to spend pursuing someone else's fantasy. To present a refreshing emotional snack, let's listen to the views of a few men who dare to say what is on their minds.

JACK

Jack is a native of Lake Forest, Illinois—a place so posh, he says, the worst thing you can ever do is to insult another guy's golf putter. Now 33 years old, Jack is an artist representative for internationally known photographers. Newly divorced, he resides in an old monastery and says his favorite form of exercise is unfolding lounge chairs.

Some of my friends can't imagine why I go out with the women I do. Many may not be described as screaming beauties, but I'm attracted to them. I mistrust any woman who doesn't like to eat. What that shows me is that all they're concerned with is the superficial. "Oh! I eat like a birrrr-d!" they say, so that someone doesn't think they are gluttons. Well, I like thinking somebody's a glutton in some respects. I think of life as a big amusement park, and I like people who think the same way and enjoy the damn thing. Hell's bells!

As far as women, I've been with itsy-bitsy things who were 4'8" and weighed 80 lbs., and I've gone out with girls who had me both in height and weight. It's the woman that matters—not her size.

KEVIN

Kevin is a Massachusetts-born poet who has become a Hollywood jack-of-all-trades, having acted and served as casting director for several motion pictures. At 6'1", blond, and good looking, Kevin fits the image of the California surfer type, but a discussion with him quickly breaks the stereotype about such men.

I've always been attracted to the classic beauties you see in Botticelli and Rubens paintings. By that I mean beautiful women with curves. Thin women might look attractive all made up in a magazine, but when a woman is without clothes, it's definitely more of a turn-on to see a voluptuous body with a great chest.

I date different kinds of women, both thin and large, and the appeal is more than just physical. If it's to be something more than a pick-up, she needs other qualities, too.

A couple of my friends edit men's magazines, but magazines like *BBW* which show sexy women in lingerie and bathing suits are a bigger turn-on to me.

Anything sexual that I can do with a thin woman can be done with a big woman, too. I'd love to go to bed with two gorgeous big women with huge chests, especially if one were blonde and the other dark-haired. And I don't care how much some guys may say they'll take nothing but a model type to bed, I could count on one hand the number of men who would refuse someone who was big and beautiful. And I think most guys worth knowing wouldn't refuse to have a long-term relationship with a big woman they fell in love with.

One of the women I used to date was not only big but she was very tall. I'm very tall, and so we were real compatible. She never had any problem drawing stares from men when we went out. Dressed in a black, lowcut dress with a flower in her hair, she could have done a Black Velvet billboard. In fact, where's my phonebook? I wonder if she's back in town yet!

ROBB

Robb is a Massachusetts-born 23-year-old who enjoys two careers. He's a top-ranked welterweight boxer and an up-and-coming fashion model. Robb once toiled in the New York Rangers hockey system.

I frequently date big women. The good thing about a large woman is that she hasn't always had to depend upon her dress size to give her a sense of pride. Big women in general move through life with a lot of pride and a cheerful attitude.

Nothing pleases me more than to see a big woman jouncing down the road with her back straight and her head up, unashamed of her size. It's a feeling of power, too, for a male to be seen in the company of a big female, a strong person. They give off more energy, or at least they *seem* to have more energy.

I find them very sexually appealing, too. There's nothing like wrapping your arms around a big woman and feeling her strong body with your hands on her back. Everyone likes physical contact and sometimes a little wrestling. A big-boned girl makes the wrestling more pleasurable.

My former girlfriend wasn't self-conscious at all about her weight. She's the one I had in mind when I said there's nothing like a big woman walking tall. She weighed more than I did, but believe me I loved our workouts.

If a guy's getting crap from other guys for going out with a big woman, I think it's mostly jealousy. I don't know too many men who aren't basically attracted to a big woman.

I like big women dressed in slacks that show off their legs, particularly if they have long legs. I like loose tops, too, that show some cleavage. I'm going out with a Swedish girl now who looks dynamite. She's taller than I am too. Size six girls are supposed to be so ladylike and petite, but they don't have half the class she does.

Men certainly don't share the bad attitude that women have toward bigness. A woman with a poor attitude is afraid to stand tall and proud. She slouches, which only makes her look as bad as she feels. If only she would stand erect and proud, it would make all the difference in the world how other people perceive her. Maybe this book and *BBW Magazine* can help big women form a different attitude about themselves.

I like a woman who can say, "Hey! This body that I'm in has two primary functions: it's to keep my brain from splattering onto the sidewalk, and the second is to make me feel good. It does neat things like eat and touch and play in the sun." It's always bothered me that if you get hung up and say this thing that's keeping my brain from splattering on the sidewalk doesn't look right by society's standards, then you can never get to the second function which is to feel good.

I'm not going to look like Robert Redford anytime in the near future any more than a big gal is suddenly going to turn into a size three. Why spend your whole life worrying about it? It's a total waste of time.

This world works on stereotypes. The stereotype for women is even more pronounced than the stereotype for men; there's much less latitude for them. A beer gut for men is even considered a sign of masculinity. But for a woman the mold is unbreakable so they must continue to wish they were a size seven fitting into a certain kind of fashion.

The real good-looking people I call the Mold People. God stamped out a couple hundred thousand of them and scattered them across the landscape. The thing wrong with good-looking people is that they've never had to work at it. You talk to them and there's nothing there because there never was any reason for them to do anything other than go around looking like an orthodontia ad. They just come

up and say, "Hai-yyye!"—and you're supposed to fall down at their feet.

Until I was 16 or 17, I was the fat kid in class. So I've seen it from that side, too. "Here comes Buffo-Boy, whooo-aaa-ooa!" While all the orthodontia people were blinding you with their Gleem smiles, you had to learn to *do* something.

It's stupid for a girl to walk into a party and want to be admired by 18 different men. Even if you're an orthodontia dream and every head does turn, what are you going to do? You can't handle 18 men. The only thing worth doing is to find one person that you enjoy being with.

We all want to be loved; we all want to be liked. The things some people will do to be liked! They'll sweat off pounds in the steamroom or they'll give up food they want. The Mold People, that's *all* they spend their time doing! Deprivation!—What a waste of life. That's no fun at all.

And what happens to the Mold People when the first wrinkle or the first accident happens? They've had nothing in life to prepare them; there's nothing behind them. They take everything at a superficial level.

DARROW

One of the hottest new comedians on television, Darrow has emerged as a foremost cult character on American college campuses. In addition, he has appeared in several motion pictures. Darrow is recently married. Here he offers his thoughts on big women.

I was attracted to my wife, who was quite heavy, the minute I met her. It wasn't *because* of her size; there was something else going on. There was a sexuality in her speech that was the most attractive thing. All guys have their preferences; her qualities just happened to hit my mark.

Every guy has his fantasy woman, but they don't always work in real life. I'm attracted to both large and small women. It all depends on how they carry themselves, how they walk, how they're put together, and what I feel from them.

Some women lose their womanly appeal because they don't *feel* attractive. If you believe that you are the sexiest chick on the planet, you can attract damn near whomever you choose. It has to do with what you think, how you feel, what you know.

100

It's all up to the woman, although one man might help give her some confidence. If he says you are a very *bad* lady and very sexual and desirable, it has nothing to do with size. It's just that somebody along the line—some guy who hates women probably—said you're nothing unless you're thin. It's self-hypnosis or maybe a mass hypnosis.

It's changing now. People are starting to admit what they like, but subconsciously they're still afraid because they've been taught that a thin woman is the most desirable woman. In today's society people *are* just larger—Period.

My mother has always been heavy. After my father died, my mother had *many* boyfriends; she attracted a lot of men. I can't remember anyone giving her pressure about weight.

She and my wife have a charismatic thing. Call it what you want; it's different for everyone. Maybe it's self-confidence.

I like cut-off jeans that show a woman's body. I love peasant clothes and the look of a well-dressed woman, too. But what attracts me the most is simplicity; that shows off the sexiness. It has nothing to do with size.

TINY

A man with an unusual occupation, Tiny makes his living as a modern day bounty hunter tracking bail skips. His notoriety has led to other jobs as a security chief and bodyguard. He himself is a big man, weighing 340 lbs. and standing 6'3". He has been the subject of articles in magazines and newspapers as well as a guest on national TV shows. His wife Jeannie is a lovely woman who fluctuates between a size 16 and 20.

You don't have to tell me about the problems of fat people. I've heard every joke there is to tell, and I know what it's like to go to school and be the butt of every cruel schoolboy who's hoping to make his reputation by making fun of the big guy.

As far as lovemaking goes, I'd say we big people are the best. We're so aware, or overaware maybe, of our weight that we take the greatest care to distribute our weight properly while making love. I've never hurt anyone in bed, and I've never been hurt in return. My experiences with big women have all been good.

I take that back. The one thing about some big women that drives me bananas is all their talk about diets. It's boring, plain and simple. If I so much as take a damn cracker to bed, my wife starts jawing about calories. I can talk till I'm blue in the jaw, but she just doesn't

101

understand that I love her exactly the way she is. I've never asked her to change, but she sees three soap operas, four movie magazines and a paperback dietbook some afternoon, and by night she's rarin' to go on some new surefire formula to lose weight. I guess it works. Whenever she goes on a diet, *I* wind up losing ten pounds.

But I think big women can be attractive, just as big men can be. Now I'm a braggart, never have been accused of being modest, and I'll tell you that since all this publicity I've gotten, there hasn't been a week go by that I haven't gotten goo-goo eyes from one female or another. You take Al Hirt, one of my idols, or Orson Welles, or I don't know, Raymond Burr—you think any of those guys are sitting alone on Saturday nights dreaming masturbatory thoughts? The same with big women. The day is going to come when big women are the sex symbols again. It's got to be. Everything else goes full cycle and comes around again. I've always believed in being ahead of the trends. In fact, the longer other men stay away from big women the better I like it. Why? There's more of 'em for Tiny.

MAX

Max is a 25-year-old photographer and filmmaker currently living among the Navaho Indians in Arizona. Of mixed German, Mexican and Indian parentage himself, Max is filming a documentary on twentieth century Native Americans. Max's work has appeared in Mother Jones, Outside, New Times, Oui *and* The Saturday Evening Post. Rolling Stone *Magazine praised his work in a collection of promising young photographers.*

My first affair was with a large-size woman. I had a real strong attraction to her. She had blonde hair, and she seemed even bigger to me because I was so small. I weighed 140 lbs. then (I'm 170 lbs. now). Since she was older—I was 18—she knew more about what to do. I knew her for quite a long time.

There was real friendship going on between us for some time, but also sexual innuendoes. Even though she was 35, we could relate easily. The sexual part was just something that kind of happened.

She was a genuinely good person as well as attractive. It's only in looking back at photos that I see her as big; at that time it was not in my mind that "Oh, this is a big person I am with."

Because I'm a photographer, I'm conscious of how people look in every way: their color, their eyes, their hair and their fashion. I appreciate all kinds of beauty in women. I'm attracted to large breasts most of all, which you often find with so-called overweight women.

These women are warm, cuddly and nice to hold. Most are very feminine with their soft curves.

Sometimes when I'm attracted to a big woman's softness and bigness, I wonder where my feelings come from because society tells me I'm wrong. Society has made some women feel so unattractive that they are intimidated when a man does come on to them sexually.

Indian women are often very large. Only among urban Indians is there any kind of putdown because they too are taking society's belief that everyone has to be skinny. Out on the reservation, places that are still natural, women are very much accepted sexually and socially when they're big.

JOHN

Chairman of the Psychology Department at a Colorado college, John says that he is "one of the dangerous breed of anachronistic males who still values chivalry, honor, principle and service." The 46-year-old Ph.D. is married and the father of two teenagers.

I am speaking as a student of human behavior, and as a professional who has worked with human beings and their joys and sorrows over a good many years. As *BBW Magazine* accomplishes its purpose—the creation of a forum for the larger woman to develop a positive self-image—this will constitute one of the major breakthroughs in psychology during the twentieth century.

I first encountered *BBW* in April of this year, and I was delighted beyond words, and candidly, just a tad jealous. Here was an obvious social need being filled. I could see that there was much more substance here than a mere fad. The editorials, the letters, the beautiful article on how to raise a "Big, Beautiful, Little Girl"—these all helped to form a picture of people being led out of a dark age. I felt in the presence of a pioneer spirit.

We all know what that "dark age" is I just referred to, particularly any of us who have grown up with the sobriquet of "Fat" or its more polite version, "Obese." There are many synonyms, some which are euphemistic, some which are straightout cruel. All of them deal with a mythical standard of physiognomy. If you pass this certain point in size you are, supposedly, what these words say. Moreover, in our society all of these words mean "ugly"—you are beyond the magic line where you are admirable for *any* quality, anymore. You are no longer respectable.

For a male it isn't all that bad. Our culture has always found a place for a "big feller"—especially since a big male is good for football, wrestling, lifting things and enforcing the playground or gang codes.

For the big girl? Loneliness.

A large woman is told over and over again that things are her own fault. You brought it upon yourself by eating too much. No excuses. You did it. You are deplorable as a human being because you eat too much. To loneliness, add self-loathing. The product of loneliness and self-loathing is depression, a real killer among human emotions.

But finally *BBW* came around and turned things the way they should be in a fresh perspective.

First, you should respect yourself for what you are right now, and realize that you have been victimized by things over which you have no control—the fashioners and developers of the mythical standard. Once you love the house in which you live, you will be ready to add touches here and there to improve it: a new hairdo, a new dress, a pair of jeans, some chic shoes, a different approach to makeup. As you do, you begin to adopt the attitude that you want to present yourself in a way that tells the world: *Here I am and I like me!*

Secondly, at last you are now able to shop for fashionable clothes in your size, designed to show you off instead of hide you. When you sport the clothes that big women aren't "supposed" to wear—you are doing your own therapy by telling the mythical standard makers to take a walk, preferably out of your way.

Third, as you begin to like and take care of yourself more and more, another surprise in store is that men are not supposed to whistle at big women, but they do. Males have not openly expressed admiration for big women because it has been part of the cultural norm not to do so. Yet deep within the mysticism of many cultures and the folklore of many countries there is admiration for the big woman. The right clothes and your own self-regard and self-respect are all you need to take advantage of this situation. Thanks to *BBW* the boys are again coming out of the weeds to be counted as your admirers.

You will likely get an abundance of cheap shots. Be ready, be persistent and tell the opposition to go to hell. Anyone who is on the cutting edge of a social change encounters this. Big, beautiful ladies!—Your time in the sun, and the moonlight, has come at last.

Myth:

FAT PEOPLE ARE UNHEALTHY.

False.

More and more scientific data is finding that doctors in recent years have greatly exaggerated the impact of extra pounds. The stress and anxiety that big people suffer because of these myths is undoubtedly more unhealthy than a pair of lovehandles.
P.S. This is my grandmother who was a size 44 and lived to be 95 years old!

7 | TAKE TWO ASPIRINS AND LOSE FIFTY POUNDS

Not so long ago in history, learned doctors were shaking sticks and howling at the moon to effect cures. Only a century ago they were attaching leeches to people's bodies to relieve them of disease. They even tried to cure tuberculosis by ordering sufferers to bear children. Author Somerset Maugham's mother died as a result of such medical sagacity. The eighteenth century cure for malaria was to burn fires. Even today doctors are not much closer when it comes to prescribing cures for the common cold, herpes simplex two, cancer and hundreds of other illnesses. In short, doctors do *not* have all the answers. Your physician may not like to hear it put this way, but he is no god. He is a service you rely upon: nothing more, nothing less.

LOOK BEFORE YOU LEAP

When choosing a doctor, shop around with no less care and educated skepticism than you use when looking for a good mechanic or any other service supplier you need. A physician is a very real man or woman with very real prejudices, a certain kind of background, personal problems, perhaps some hair loss that's causing trauma, and whatever material he's managed to retain from medical school. When he hangs up his shingle, his final grades are never posted on a wall to see his strong and weak subjects.

111

When you come to the doctor's office, you want him to fix you up. After all, he is a 'body mechanic,' so to speak. You're there to head off problems or because you've broken down. Yet bodies are not as simple as cars. Cadillacs, Fords and Toyotas are more or less built the same. The spare parts come in clearly labeled boxes. Unfortunately, your friendly neighborhood sawbones can't go into a backroom and fumble around for rebuilt spleens and pancreases.

Another thing: What the doctor is really giving when he "doctors" you in his *opinion* on what he thinks is the problem. Doctors, of course, have been known to make mistakes. A diagnosed tumor in a BBW reader turned out five months later to be an eight pound ten ounce baby boy. We've all heard the horror story of the impossibly heavy woman whom doctors told had a glandular problem—until they discovered a 180 lb. tumor imbedded in her body. All the more reason to get a second and even a third opinion if major surgery is required.

Moreover, we patients are entitled to respect. We pay an awfully high fee for a doctor's services. In addition, you come to *him* for your service, not he to you. To get him to help you, there are times when you, the customer, must forego up to an hour of your own time to wait meekly in a waiting room because he overbooks in case of a no-show. He knows that his time is money; he doesn't always feel the same about your time.

DON'T GET MAD, GET EVEN

I have a 300 lb. friend. Whenever she's made to fuss and fidget too long in a doctor's office, she smiles sweetly at those in the waiting room and then drops a bombshell.

"I'm so worried," she says demurely. "The doctor told me to *gain* four pounds this week, and I've only put on three!"

Finally, we should not turn over hard cash to become the victim of a weight bigot dressed in the regalia of an expert.

As *BBW's* interviews and questionnaires have overwhelmingly indicated, fat people invariably fall prey to the malice with forethought of many doctors who find our weight a personal affront—or at least that is the impression formed by the tone some doctors adopt.

Many otherwise concerned physicians treat fat people without courtesy, without dignity, without respect. We must stop all such practices. Would we take similar abuse from a maid, plumber, electrician, roofer, or any other professional whose services we purchase? Don't buy this "I'm only doing it for your own good" jazz either. You can suggest anything you want for my own good, doctor. That's why I'm paying your lofty fees. Only suggest what you will with consideration, with respect, with kindness, and with the understanding that I have *employed* your service.

We consumers have meekly accepted horrendous behavior from doctors who point their finger toward the door like some biblical patriarch and command: "Either lose 50 lbs. or don't come back because I don't want you dying in *my* office!" What, I've often wondered, are such doctors so angry about—the fact that we might die or the prospect of carrying our carcass out of his office?

DELAY CAN BE FATAL

In all seriousness, because fat women have been subjected to previous bad treatment, many delay seeing a physician for preventative check-ups (such as a pap smear), or for minor annoyances such as cysts. Too often, complications develop as a result of patient's reluctance to face a scolding. Because you're sick of their rudeness, don't risk your health.

One reader took a merciless drubbing for having an ingrown toenail. The Hippocratic representative told her, "If you had 250 lbs. pressing down on you, you'd be ingrown too!" She felt real anger and disappointment; it would take nothing less than need of amputation to get her back in a doctor's office again.

Who wants to be treated for a headache by being told to take two aspirins and lose 50 lbs.? There are doctors who blame every ailment upon weight without a single shred of actual physical evidence. "I know you broke your leg skiing," we are told, "but you wouldn't have fallen down if you weren't so fat." Skinny people, we all know, never fall on a slope.

In fact, doctors seem miffed oftentimes when you come away with a clean bill of health. After all, what right do *you* have to be fat *and* healthy? Instead of beaming and presenting you with the good news, they glare and warn you that while you may be all right now, you're likely to drop dead before sunset. In an excellent article entitled "An Open Letter to My Doctor," *BBW* writer Joanna Nemes says several doctors have told her she suffers from a "diseased state" they refer to as obesity. She understands their duty to inform patients whose fatness they consider a threat to their health. But too many doctors seem adamantly opposed not only to the "disease," but to the people who "suffer" it. Because she's received expert advice smacking in moral judgment and smug rejection, Nemes has resisted seeing a

113

doctor for over two years and has friends who've not gone in five years. She wishes that doctors who are prejudiced against fat people would list this bias on their shingle (*No fat people allowed!*), or disqualify themselves the way judges do, and treat just the thin people they care so much more about.

DEMAND QUALITY TREATMENT

It isn't only words that hurt us. Sometimes a physician's carelessness does more stress-related damage than sticks and stones. How many times have doctors deduced an erroneous blood pressure reading because they've insisted on fitting a regular-sized cuff on a large person's arm? Every physician is supposed to have an oversized cuff, and probably has, but some nurses are too lazy or indifferent to locate one. Often the patient is unaware that a large cuff exists. Insensitivity in medical offices may extend to fitting a large person into a regular-sized dressing gown or onto an undersized examining table.

When you add up your doctor bills for the year, you start figuring he can afford to cover your big beautiful bod with something more than a skimpy dressing gown. Why not just tell him that as a good businessman it behooves him to spring for a gown that fits his large-size customers.

Nurses too must be handled as people who are offering you a service. Some are angels of mercy and deserve your gratitude. Others are cold-hearted, unfeeling shrews who should be complained about at once.

You also have a right to privacy. There is no need to be weighed in a room with other patients watching if this bothers you. Head off embarrassing situations at the pass by quietly insisting for the preferential treatment which is reflected in your bill anyway.

YOU BETTER SHOP AROUND

Shop around to find a doctor who, together with his nurses, is sympathetic to all his patients. He may *advise* you, that as an obese person, you run a greater risk of tissue damage and bleeding during surgery. That's part of his job and is required to satisfy his malpractice insurance. However, once you have informed him that you are comfortable with your weight and expect to be at this weight in the long-term future, he must deal with your medical needs as an individual. You owe him no false promise that you'll reduce. You owe

114

him no apology for your weight. You owe him no obligation to listen to any antagonism toward fat people.

You don't have to accept everything a doctor says just because he said it. I don't want to be told that fatness *leads* to high blood pressure because there is *no* hard evidence to prove that statement. I don't want to be told that I'm going to get diabetes because of my weight when thin people also suffer adult-onset diabetes. As MIT professor William Bennett, M.D., and *American Health* Managing Editor Joel Gurin, state in their fascinating book, *The Dieter's Dilemma,* " 'desirable' weight is a statistical fiction." Although several time-consuming and well-researched studies to find a correlation between cardiovascular disease and weight gain have turned up highly contradictory and inconclusive findings. For now, at least, any doctor who states with "certainty" that obesity "causes" heart attacks is just plain uninformed. Ditto with diabetes and high blood pressure unless new studies prove otherwise. Dr. Bennett calls medical profession condemnation of fat as a disease causer "premature" at best.

Two *BBW* readers who are registered nurses, Morgan Greenwood and Mary Olson, insist that a doctor who fails to accommodate himself to your needs does not deserve your business. If he shows a hostile or condescending attitude, put on your clothes and march out of his office. As a consumer, you have the *right* to expect reasons for a diagnosis, clarification for anything you do not understand, and at all times, dignified professional treatment. The medical profession has plenty of capable, warm-hearted physicians concerned about the well-being of their patients who have no ego-serving need to demean any of their clients.

FIND A CURE FOR WHAT AILS YOU

On the other hand, if you have a weight-connected disease, you should do something about it.

My husband Ray suffers from diabetes. He weighed 260 lbs. when he was informed that he had the disease; then he lost weight upon his doctor's orders. At his top weight, Ray was every bit as sexy to me as back in his Broadway days when he weighed 190 lbs. He hadn't changed in my eyes one bit, but I wanted him to live. He had to diet, and I supported that decision wholeheartedly.

There was no choice. His diabetes was up, his blood pressure was out of sight, and his triglicerides were off the wall. If he didn't diet, Saint Peter would be outfitting him for an oversized set of wings. The day he left the doctor's office, Ray went on a diet. Not, however, on the doctor's diet. He didn't touch red meat, he laid off bread, and he kept his carbohydrate intake low for two weeks. When it came time to visit the doctor, he hadn't lost a single ounce. The doctor was upset and berated him for not going on the prescribed diet. But after taking tests, the doctor found that Ray's sugar count was *down* 259 points, his blood pressure was in the normal range, and his triglyceride count was down to 110. In addition, he was wearing pants that he had not worn in two years. The doctor shook his head and admitted the diet was succeeding *despite* those numbers on a scale indicating that he was eating in his usual way.

Ray eventually lost weight, but if you looked at *what* he was eating those first two weeks, and in what portions, he should have dropped ten pounds. My theory is this: back in the caveman days our ancestors learned to deal with famine. Their bodies learned to use whatever food was available in the thriftiest way possible. In the survival of the fittest, bodies that couldn't adjust simply died out.

YOU CAN'T FOOL MOTHER NATURE

Now, however, in the 1980's, we have an era when slimness is in fashion. No longer is it a case of survival for the fittest and fattest. But the human body is an evolved mechanism that doesn't know intuitively that *Women's Wear Daily* thinks it's supposed to be thin as a rail. It still functions the way it did back in our ancestors' day, with a little man or homunculus inside us regulating the controls. Your body doesn't know that you are dieting to fit into your St. Germaine jeans. It thinks there's a *famine* going on out there, and prepares itself to pull out all stops for survival. The little man in the control tower puts out the word which says the body must use food in a thrifty way, and because all of us have dieted many, many times before, our bodies make more thrifty use of less food than someone who has never dieted.

A more scientific hypothesis is provided by Dr. William Bennett of MIT University. The medical doctor has a theory that one's body really cares how much energy, i.e. fat, it has stored. He calls this constant striving of the body to reach a level of fat its "setpoint." A setpoint changes with age, but it is fairly constant under constant conditions. "A diet doesn't change the setpoint," says Dr. Bennett. "What happens is that the dieter sets up a struggle between his or her conscious effort (to diet) and the unconscious mechanism of the setpoint. The setpoint is perfectly capable of making the dieter quite miserable with constant hunger, depression, irritability, lethargy

116

eventually, and always pressure to eat." Hence, he concludes, it is this unconscious mechanism which forces " most of us to give in" and weigh what Mother Nature intended.

To put it in simpler terms—Just as gasoline fuels a car's engine, food fuels our bodies. It is a simple fact that some of us have larger fuel tanks than others. And try as *we* may—by dieting—we may fill our tanks only half way. When that happens our engine starts to buck. It demands its full measure. So sooner or later (mostly sooner) we are off our diets and back to "filling her up." Only many times we compensate to make up for the time we were running on half a tank.

BEATING THE SYSTEM

No matter what the reason is for your being big, you are a consumer of medical services. Learn to become a wise consumer and demand only those services you wish. Don't offend the doctor necessarily; just shop as wisely as you do for any other expensive service. For example, I once made an appointment to be tested specifically for diabetes. I did not request a check-up, merely a blood and urine test. The nurse seemed taken aback, but she spoke to the doctor, and I was led into a waiting room. I explained to the doctor the symptoms I was concerned about and made it very clear that I wanted nothing more than a blood and urine test for diabetes.

Almost grudgingly he ordered the tests. When I finished, my bill was $117. Shocked, I asked the nurse to explain the charges, which were written in "doctorese" and unintelligible to me. The office visit was $29 (OK). The urine test was $8 (fine and dandy), and the broad spectrum blood test was $80 (not fine OR dandy at all!).

"I will not pay for a multi-purpose test," I said. "I requested clearly a test for blood sugar, and that is all I intend to pay for. If I went to a garage to fix a flat in my left rear tire, you wouldn't bill me for the other three tires too. Please tell this to the doctor."

The nurse looked at me as if I were from outer space, but she took off like a roadrunner to tell the physician. Five minutes later, quite obviously put off by my audacity, she said the doctor would do as I requested. The blood test bill went down from $80 to $12! I left feeling much more appeased than I would had I sulked out after paying the unnecessary charges. Not that I blamed the doctor for wanting to go to Europe every year; I just don't want to send him singlehandedly.

P.S. I didn't have diabetes.

P.P.S. I changed doctors.

8 | TO YOUR HEALTH

When I was 12 years old, I enrolled in a health spa. Today I never would have been allowed to join. Because a pre-teen's body is so malleable and unformed, a 12-year-old isn't even allowed to receive a professional massage. Back then, however, this now-defunct New York reducing salon willingly accepted my membership fee.

My clearest memory is of me inserted between two rollers which obviously had been devised by the Marquis de Sade of the health club world. These rollers kneaded and pummeled me as though my body were a batch of cookie dough. If this experience wasn't frightening and demeaning enough, the fact that I was by far the youngest person there made me feel out of place. In addition, I was nearly traumatized by the constant awareness that the only reason I was enrolled in this place of torture was because I was fat.

There was no one to blame for my predicament but myself. My mother certainly didn't force me to attend. She thought I looked perfect just the way I was. My schoolmates weren't putting undue pressure upon me. If they did, my patented arm-wrenching hammer-lock would have made them cry "uncle" quick enough.

No, the problem (if there *was* a problem), was that even at this early age, the movie, book and magazine industry had gotten to me. Physically I wasn't what the All-American heartthrob female was supposed to look like, and since self-help even then was the media rage, I decided that I would self-help myself into an hourglass figure.

119

Always there was a carrot dangling before me, and this was just one more attempt to snatch off a bite.

EXERCISE IS NOT A DIRTY WORD, EITHER

I heartedly endorse exercise for health and enjoyment. No matter how big you are, beautiful woman, the fact of weight should not deter you in the least from taking pleasure with your body.

If, for example, you love to play volleyball, don't mope on the sidelines at your favorite beach or resort because you're conscious of your size. When you want to play, just stroll right up and enjoy the fun. To hesitate because you think your thighs are too chunky is to deny yourself a wholesome, healthy form of entertainment.

Don't you think it is a foolish waste of time to worry about what other people think of your body? Believe me, they spend a lot less time worrying about your weight than you do. It's a form of egotism—albeit a negative form—when you assume that anyone is paying intense concern over your size. Think about it. How many of your waking hours do you spend contemplating someone else's size? Even if someone has put on or dropped 30 lbs., you note the fact mentally and then move on to something else. Why then do you suppose anyone would be pre-occupied with your weight? You are important only to yourself and those who love or depend upon you. Anyone else forgets about you the second they've paid you a passing glance.

Therefore, there is no earthly reason why you, as a big person, shouldn't get out to enjoy a sport or exercise the same way that thin people do. How many times have you refused an invitation to play tennis or go for a swim because you're afraid people won't approve of you in a brief outfit? Even if you're not the type who looks fantastic in frilled underwear, why shouldn't you enjoy hitting an ace just as much as the next person? If you were a good player when thin, you'll still do your share of winning—on the court. And even if your score reads "love" all day, don't blame your loss on your weight. Just enjoy the competition and do your best.

LISTEN TO AN EXPERT

Author Karen Lustgarten, herself just under six feet and voluptuous, is a well-publicized promoter of exercise and sports for large-size persons. Her credits include *The Complete Guide to a Dynamic Body*, which is an indispensible addition to any exercise enthusiast's library.

"The body needs to exercise," she maintains. "That's what your muscles are for—to help you move purposefully and gracefully. Many aches and pains come about from a lack of exercise which has nothing to do with size. It has to do with simple needs of the body and mind. It also relieves stress and anxiety. But exercise has to be fun or you'll quit. It has to be so exciting that it makes you smile while you do it. The rewards have to be so fantastic that you gain the impetus to continue."

For large-size women, Lustgarten especially approves of walking and swimming. "Brisk walking is the *best* exercise," she insists. "It's enjoyable because the scenery changes constantly and you can do it anywhere except at night in a dark alley. The best walking involves perspiring deeply and taking just as long a stride as you can. It doesn't strain or stress your muscles where you put yourself in danger of pulling a muscle as you would in some sports. Besides, it's convenient and cheap. All you need is a pair of running shoes. Swimming is another good exercise which is an ideal way to feel good, especially when combined with walking."

HOW TO FEEL LIKE A BBW

BBW writer Beverly Hutchins Jordan is one who advocates exercise, but not the huff-and-puff grueling calisthenics that so many of us have undergone in an attempt to peel off the pounds. She's talking about graceful stretches and movements that feel good.

There are many ways to incorporate movement to your daily life. If you spend hours seated at a desk, take a stretching break to relieve tension in your back and shoulders. Or, if your job requires that you stand for long stretches of time, take a periodic break to rotate your ankles and flex and point your feet, raise up on your toes and flex your knees. Whenever you have to pick up small objects from the floor, bend at the waist, keeping your legs straight. Really s-t-r-e-t-c-h for that item on the top shelf. When you're sitting at a table, stretch your arms as high as you can, then reach from side to side. Tie your shoelaces the hard way: Facing a wall, table or bar, lift each leg to at least waist level, press your foot against the wall (or rest it on the table or bar) for balance and stretch your torso and arms to meet your foot. Use your imagination as well as your body!

Just as BBW's come in all shapes, colors and sizes, there are various forms of exercise. Jogging, walking, dance, karate, yoga, gymnastics,

121

weight training, swimming, skating—choose an activity that you'll enjoy and get moving! Just be sure to note the following!

1) If you have any health problems (hypertension, heart problems, diabetes, varicose veins, etc.) check with an M.D. before beginning a serious exercise routine. If you get the old song-and-dance about losing weight, simply say that you are concerned about feeling good not reaching some smaller size. If your doctor really doesn't understand remind him/her of the 96 percent recidivism rate of weight reduction programs and stress your commitment to feeling good about your body at any weight.

2) Start slowly, especially if you haven't exercised since high school gym classes. Try easy movements, limiting repetitions of any movement until your body tells you you're ready for more. The aim of exercise is to provide energy, not exhaustion.

3) Exercise does no good when it is done sporadically. For starters find 15 minutes each day to perform your movements. Bedtime is especially nice for yoga or other simple, relaxing movements. Or try waking up earlier to start your day with energizing exercise. Extend the length of your exercise time as your body becomes accustomed to movement.

4) If you don't like solitary workouts, or you need the stimulation of others to keep you going, join a group or start one yourself! Don't worry about being the biggest woman in the class. If you don't let your size inhibit you, then no one else will comment. Everyone is there for the same reason as you—to feel good.

Don't listen to the diet fakes who offer to teach you exercises to "trim down your fat stomach/thighs/hips, etc." Movement is so much more than calisthenics. Look for a convenient group with a skilled, knowledgeable leader. You don't need fancy machines or scales all over the room.

After a few weeks of regular exercise, you'll notice your posture and walk will improve, your muscles will feel tighter and you'll be more flexible. You'll feel much more graceful and will be able to do more without tiring as easily. This is something that you do for yourself—for the joy it gives you to use your body for its own pleasure—and not because you're trying to fit someone else's image of what you should be. After all, whom should you try to please— Richard Simmons or yourself?

There is one other form of exercise you won't want to do without once you start. The expert, Karen Lustgarten, calls them "sexy exercises for partners only." Says the aptly named Lustgarten: "They help you to arrive at a position that lets you accomplish things you couldn't do without a partner."

Amen to that!

Myth:
FAT WOMEN DON'T CARE ABOUT FASHION — JUST COMFORT.

False.

Taste does not shrink in direct proportion to body enlargement. We can tell the difference between fashionable and frumpy.

9 | PUTTING ON THE GLITZ

Years ago when my husband was travelling, he stopped at Marshall Field's in Chicago to buy me a surprise gift in the lingerie department.

"I want to buy the sheerest nightgown you have," he said to the salesgirl.

"All right," she replied. "What size?"

"I don't know what size."

"How much does your wife weigh?" she asked helpfully.

"About 150 lbs." (Remember, I said this was years ago.)

SHEER DELIGHT

She stepped back in shock and went silently to the stockroom to see what she could show him. The girl seemed startled that he'd want to view the exposed body of a woman who weighed 150 lbs.

It took her a while to find anything. After all, for many, many years all clothes manufacturers tended to share her prejudice. I'm convinced that nightgowns are created by size six designers who perceive that a big woman is either sexless or so ashamed of her body that naturally, she'd want it covered up. Or if *she* didn't, her mate certainly did. When that Chicago salesgirl finally returned, she was convinced a crazy man was making a purchase because he held it up to make sure it was sheer enough.

There's one other detail to this story I've left out. When Ray gave me that sheer nightgown, it took every bit of courage I could muster to slip into it—even for my husband. I was so programmed to dislike my body that I had trouble understanding that Ray not only accepted me, but actually loved me as I was. Like many BBWs today, I had still not taken responsibility for using clothing as my language. I was conditioned to feel this way because I was fat. It took me many years to learn that I had the right to be a selective consumer, choosing only products which pleased me from the fashion world (the third largest industry in the country, after food and steel).

ME ON ED SULLIVAN'S SHOW

The nightgown incident occurred around the same time as one of the greatest thrills in my singing career: an appearance on Ed Sullivan's *Toast of the Town*. I was to sing my hit song "Careless." I remember looking at myself dressed in an ultra-fancy gown once owned by Patti Page (every seam of which had been let out)— thinking that I had put something over on everybody. No one in the mass of humanity who watched the show that night, I decided, could detect my deep, dark secret. I was a size 12.

After I had finished my number, I ran out amid applause to the wings where Ray was looking quite proud as he waited for me. Once again, I feared weight had won over talent. I didn't ask, "How did I sing?" You know what I said? *"Did I look too fat?!"*

COLOR ME HAPPY

Always I worried about finding clothes that would *slenderize* me. How I hate that word "slenderize!" A piece of clothing is either going to make me look attractive or unattractive. Period. You can paint me navy blue from head to toe, and the most I'll look is five pounds thinner. At 200 lbs., five pounds doesn't mean an awful lot to me! However, I am in ecstasy when I find a color that makes me happy and lets my heart sing.

When a saleslady tries to sell you a dress which will be slenderizing, look her straight in the eye and say: "Sweetheart! Unless your name is Merlin the Magician, you aren't going to slenderize me. What

you *can* do is find something that makes me look fabulous—*now!*—just as I am."

The only hard and fast rule for shopping is to throw out all advice from so-called experts who give you hard and fast rules.

HOW TO SHOP

However, I do have a few suggestions on how to shop. You can take them with a grain of salt—unless, of course, you're on a salt-free diet.

1.) USE YOUR EYES. We got fat, we didn't get stupid. If you look at a well-designed garment that makes your heart skip a beat with pleasure, chances are that other people will share your sentiments exactly.

2.) USE YOUR MIRROR. A mirror isn't going to make you fatter *or* thinner. Don't be afraid of seeing a *big* woman in the reflection. *Do* be afraid to see a big, *dowdy*-looking woman staring back at you, just as you should be afraid to see a *skinny*, dowdy person there. This has nothing to do with fat.

3.) USE YOUR HEART. Let your heart tell you that it's all right to wear bright orange, or a huge picture hat, or even a string bikini if it makes *you* happy. Whose permission should you request to give yourself pleasure?

4.) The most important advice of all! *TELL YOUR SIZE SEVEN FRIEND TO SHUT HER MOUTH!*

INVESTMENT BUYING

When you shop for clothes, go with the positive attitude that you *deserve* beautiful fashions. Don't just settle for what's there. Clothing costs a fortune whether you take what's there or reach for the moon. Not just large-size clothing, but *all* clothing is expensive today. You hear a lot of talk consequently these days about so-called "Investment Buying," or long-term buying. In the past, if you needed a sweater for a fun occasion which required nothing overly special, you might fork over $7.98 for something to last the night. No longer. Today even a ho-hum sweater can cost $35, a hefty (excuse the pun!) sum for short-haul usage. Few of us can afford to *throw* money away today, regardless of our incomes. The new philosophy says to invest an

additional $25 or $50 in a sweater with quality workmanship. That way you have something pretty which is built to last.

QUALITY COUNTS

You can't go wrong with pure materials like cottons, silks and wools, or even blends of synthetics and pure fibers. The initial price is more, but you'll get better, longer wear, and you'll look classier too. Why blow your budget on ten things you'll only donate to a thrift store in six months when you can have three things you'll love and admire for years?

Clothes portray your body language. They don't necessarily "make" the man or woman, but they do help or hinder you in business and personal relationships. Before you utter a single word when meeting someone new, your external appearance has already spoken for you. Since this is your only time around in life, unless you seriously believe in reincarnation, when you see something you'd love to wear, then dammit, buy it! If you see a dress with decolletage you adore—even if it's cut right down to the navel, at least try it on. Don't stand there sniveling and lamenting about what "so-and-so" will think. To hell with so-and-so. What do *you* want? Assuming you're not planning to wear your new low-cut dress to the minister's reception, why shouldn't you make yourself happy by treating yourself to it?

TIMES THEY ARE A-CHANGING

Remember how big women used to shop? We used to visit store after store looking for *anything* acceptable. Forget about style. We never dreamed that we'd find it.

When we located a blouse that didn't look too, too terrible, we bought it in three or four different colors. It wasn't pleasure buying, and it certainly wasn't fashion. I mean, how exciting *is* it to wear the same thing day after day? Forget about a perfect fit! A perfect fit was what you threw if the salesgirl was more sarcastic than usual.

Today, thank God, times are a-changing. While large-size people must spend more time shopping than small-size people, you can always get what you need even if you can't always get what you want.

Not that you won't encounter clothing that is incredibly ugly. You still will try on clothes that look all right on a hanger, but are so ill-made they make you want to explode!

More than once I've heard myself scream: "How could anyone *admit* designing this? The sleeves are down to my knees, the shoulders are down around the elbows, and the print must have been conjured up during an opium flashback." Who was the fit model—a gorilla?

It *is* possible to find some good, beautifully made clothes with style. You have to search, learn to rely on a few informed stores, and not discourage easily. Think of yourself as a person with special physical characteristics, such as a concert violinist who needs custom gloves to cover her long fingers. That way the shopping seems more intriguing and less wearisome.

Many store buyers, unfortunately, still live in the Dark Ages, and I mean that *literally*. They think that navy blue polyester pant suits are the surefire answer to any question involving large-size women. I'm surprised we were never treated to navy blue, polyester negligees!

BULLET-PROOF POLYESTER

I'm not knocking all polyesters—They can look good, especially when blended with pure fibers such as cotton, wool and silk. It's the double-knit, bullet-proof kind—and their overuse that makes me see red.

How did the whole double knit myth get started? Well, it stretched everywhere, and it was the veritable queen of wash-and-wear (except for white, which turned murky gray regardless of what detergent you used. In fact, white polyester might better have been termed wash-and-*don't* wear!).

Most important, double-knit polyester was fairly inexpensive. Since "everyone" knows that big women hate themselves, they certainly wouldn't indulge themselves by spending money on quality clothing. Whenever I bought a polyester goodie, it was on sale, since I never liked spending more than 12 bucks on buying what I hated. I think my mentality was wrongly perceived by fashion manufacturers and store buyers. They concluded that as soon as you got fat, you got poor. They also felt that all big women were concerned with was comfort—so double-knit, bullet-proof, polyester filled the bill—and filled the bill and filled the bill, ad nauseum.

Back when we big women did wear a size 12, 14, 16 or 18 (after all, we weren't *born* a size 22!), we *did* buy pure wools, cottons and silks. Manufacturers came to the conclusion, however, that as soon as we passed a size 18, we were supposed to skip merrily into polyester heaven. Pour quoi, pray tell? How is it they deduced—as I've said before—that we got fat, *ergo* we got stupid?

134

We big women must combat the fashion world's madness. To minimize the frustration we feel about limited fashion availability, we must educate ourselves in how to shop.

SEEK PROFESSIONAL ADVICE

Walk into the large-size department or specialty store and "case the joint." Walk around, look at the other customers, check out the sales staff. Ask them, "What's *really* terrific?" You can't inspect *every* rack in *every* store, and you might miss something. Occasionally something you observe on a rack may look so-so, but a sharp salesperson has seen it magically transform other women into "knockouts" when worn.

It's not necessary to wait for a large-size saleswoman to free herself from another customer if small-size staffers are available. Some tiny ladies truly understand the large-size market and are quite helpful, compassionate beings. Some big women seem more prejudiced against fellow large women than any size three. In other words, the generalization that only a large-size saleswoman should work in a large-size department just doesn't carry any weight.

After the saleslady has played her hand, excuse yourself politely so that you can take time to compare and reflect. Never allow anyone to rush you or to yawn at your shoulder while you make a decision.

If there is something specific you want to see, ask if it's available. If you request a sexy, black nightgown, and the clerk comes back with something more appropriate for a banker's wake, be thankful that you know where *her* head is at. You're on your own, kid!

SHOP IN COMFORT

You should always shop in comfort. There will inevitably be many stops before you're plopped back on your sofa with your shoes off. Wear an outfit that is easy to get on and off. No matter what your size, when you have to unfasten 29 buttons, a belt, necklace, and 16 other accessories, you're going to get tired and crabby in short order. Make sure your hairdo is kept simple so that you don't have to fuss with it after every change. However, I always put on my full makeup so that I won't have to guess how the clothes will "really" look on me when I actually wear them to go out. Also, if you ordinarily wear a girdle, put one on to assure a proper fit.

FORTUNE FAVORS THE BOLD

I have seen many big women look marvelous in furry coats that had a lot of bulk to them. If your size seven friend saw you fingering a coat like that on the rack; she'd probably ask if you were trying to look like a polar bear. But what does she know—or what do *you* know—until you try it on? Maybe you *will* look like an Arctic mammal's mommy, but just maybe you'll make a statement about yourself that is damn imposing. Frankly, unless you're out to socialize more than to shop, I'd recommend going alone. Unless your slim friend has lost 100 lbs. last weekend, she doesn't know beans about what you should wear.

However, if shopping alone is no fun and you *must* take along a size seven friend, warn her ahead of time that you expect her to hold her opinions (as well as her own packages) unless *you* request them. She can have lunch with you and cheer you on, but she cannot pick out your clothes.

STUDY *BBW*

If you have a problem deciding what to buy, then pull out the latest edition of *BBW* or *any* fashion magazine. You don't have to approve of their philosophy to learn from their photos and models. Or you can go to Bergdorf's, Georgio's or any other chic boutique to check out *not* what's on the racks but what's on their customer's backs. If you can find an item in your size, anything a skinny person can wear a big person can wear. For example, there's no reason why a thin girl can wear a thick belt and you can't if there's one available to complete an outfit and *you* like it.

BREAK THE RULES

The hard and fast rules we big people have accepted as gospel are only so much hot helium. *Dark clothes make you look thinner*, they insist. Ha! Dark clothes make you look boring. *Vertical stripes make you look thinner*. Nope, you'll just look like a big woman wearing vertical stripes and no more. Nothing makes you slimmer except being slimmer. Nothing makes you fatter except being fatter.

The list of prohibitive "no-no's" is equally false. *Never tuck in a blouse!*—That will make you look thinner. Sorry! That will make you look pregnant. I went around looking pregnant for 20 years. Flowing caftans are synonomous with "fat lady" costumes manufactured by our supposed couturier, Omar the Tentmaker.

Are you among those who have never tucked in a blouse since the day you reached the pound of no return? Listen to me a second! When you're in that store's dressing room, you're all alone. No one will ever know. So just for kicks, go on and tuck in your blouse.

And while we're on the subject of tucking in our blouses, do *not*, I repeat, do not try tucking in your blouse while wearing polyester, pull-on pants. It looks terrible. I know it, and you know it. That's why we always wore our blouses on the outside—to cover our bellies. Right?

Pull-on polyester pants hug your body. They show every lump and every bump and grind we have. Pants should *not* hug your body. They should cover your frame and fall from your body in a graceful way. The only thing that should hug your body is your underwear— or someone you like very much!

Pants should fall in a straight line. So if you've never had a pair of pants with a waistline, a zipper and yes, *pleats*, please, oh please try some on. Pleats can be your best friend. Once you have on a pair of pleated pants, try tucking your blouse in. I really think you'll be surprised—not at how thin you look—but at how good you look.

I can hear the arguments already. After all, I've argued them myself. "Oh no! My stomach is too big." Or maybe it's your thighs, breasts, hips or rib cage. There's always a reason you shouldn't try something new. The Wright Brothers heard thousands.

Once you've made your excuses, ignore them. Grab hold of that blouse and tuck it in. The worst thing that can happen is that you'll hate it. In that case, what just went in can come out equally easy. But what happens if you *do* like it? Well, you've taken an irreversible step toward discarding the fat-lady costume syndrome.

"Carole," a big lady once said to me, "*I* can't wear a belt because *I* don't have a waistline."

"Sweetheart!" I said, "*Everyone* has a waistline. Just bend over— wherever you crack, *that's* your waistline!"

Maybe our midsections are five times bigger than Nancy Reagan's, but it is an undeniable fact that we do have a waist. If we want to wrap a belt around our midsections, who is so all-powerful as to tell us that we can't?

LONELY SHADES OF GRAY

What about colors? At long last we have some choices. Still, some women are reluctant to move with the new flow. A woman once

approached me dressed totally in gray. Even her hair was gray, which made her appearance completely washed out. "I don't think it's quite *proper* for a woman my size to wear colors," she sniffed. Obviously, she hoped to melt inconspicuously into a crowd.

Her lack of logic bothered me. Does she think a big woman can't be seen because she is wearing gray? What does she mean by not "quite proper?" Whom are we offending? Is there a law that says any woman over 190 lbs. will earn a misdemeanor for wearing chartreuse? Not proper, indeed! I have black, brown and navy outfits hanging in my own closet. They become profane only when you won't don other hues because you erroneously believe dark colors make you look slimmer.

Think about it. If you like colors because they make your head and heart happy, they make the people who see you feel good too. Would you stop any other person on this globe from wearing an outfit that gives them pleasure? No, of course not! But a big woman will time and time again stop the single most important person in her life. Herself!

THAT'S ABOUT THE SIZE OF IT

When I had outgrown the size 20 ranks, it took me six months before I could figure out my new sizes in the Women's Department. One day I spotted a jeans rack sized 32 to 44. I strolled up on my own because I dreaded having a saleslady's critical eyes roaming over my body as if it were a map of the great Gobi desert. Worse, I hated the thought of watching her whip out a tape measure to dazzle me with numbers. Since my daughter Lori, who is a size five, wears a 29 jean, I deduced that a size 32 jean would be too small. (Not quite an Einsteinian exercise in logic either!) I tried on a size 44, which promptly slid off my hips to the floor—a not unpleasant experience since nothing had ever fallen off me before but earrings.

Then I tried on a size 40 which didn't slide off, but which I could take off without unzipping. Sizes 38 and 36 clearly were too large also. I called over a saleslady at last. She informed me that she was out of 32's and 34's. I informed her, before leaving, that I was out of patience.

The next time out shopping, I was looking for a dress. Knowing that a size 20 was too small, I thought I'd try a 20½. (After all, I had gained 15 lbs., not 50.) Wrong again. The waist hovered just below my chest, as if my midsection had been surgically removed. "All right," I sighed, "let me backtrack." I moved toward the size 18½

141

HALF-SIZE DRESS
15¾" from base of neck to waist.

FULL-SIZE DRESS
17¾" from base of neck to waist.

section. No dice! The neck was the only part that fit. The shoulders and hips were too big and too small respectively. The waist again was just below my chest.

I looked into the mirror totally perplexed. I've always had an hourglass figure, even if over the years it had gained a little time. I've never had any clothing altered. "I guess I'm between sizes," I concluded. "Too small for a 20½, too big for an 18½."

I left the store in confusion. Although I had sought help, no saleslady ever disclosed the carefully guarded secret that large-sizes and half-sizes were different.

The secret—as I learned the hard way—is that half-sizes are for short and/or short-waisted women. At 5'7", and definitely not short-waisted, I turned or *tried* turning to large-size dresses. In fact, what I turned to was empty racks.

Retailers offer half-sizes instead of large-sizes because they sell more half-sizes. Of course, they sell more! They sell more because there are virtually *no* large-size dresses. It's like a Cadillac dealer boasting he sells more Sevilles than used VW's. When a woman must have a dress, she'll buy a half-size opposed to nothing. But when she raises her arms, she runs the risk of looking like her kneecaps have been soldered to her armpits.

When will the dress manufacturers commit themselves to large-size as opposed to half-size dresses? Large-size women cannot "Say 'Yes' to a Dress" (the National Dress Council slogan) when the waist is up under our arms. Manufacturers wrongly have concluded that "big women won't wear dresses," instead of conceding *they* are not making the *right* dresses. Even half-size designs are styled for Grandma Moses' grandma—great for plowing but not for playing.

FASHION FORTITUDE

However, most of us have been guilty too of not taking a chance. We make up our minds before we try something on. "Oh! That would never look good on me," we say. Or we mutter, "There are *no* pants which will fit my stomach and waistline that don't leave room for a whole 'nother person in the legs. I knew *that* five years ago."

Well, times fortunately have changed. To be accurate, times are changing in the large-size fashion field by the hour, let alone the last five years. You owe it to yourself to try on things you were told you never should wear and never had an opportunity to wear. "You have nothing to fear but fear itself," rotund statesman Franklin D. Roosevelt once said. He did not say, "You have nothing to fear but *fat* itself."

WHAT'S IN STORE?

A vacation is upcoming. You've got a hot date. You're looking to change the way you strut your stuff. You've got a fistful of dollars or a credit card burning a hole in your pocket. You've decided to go shopping. Where?

FROM HERE TO EQUALITY

Most major department stores have large-size departments. Among my favorites is *Macy's*, both in San Francisco and New York. This is a store that made a commitment right from the beginning, giving plenty of floor space and elbow room to large-size fashions and its shoppers.

There is also the *Bon* in Seattle, *Joslins* in Denver, *Blocks* in Indianapolis, *Higbees* in Cleveland, *Nordstroms* in Salt Lake City, Portland and Southern California and a store-within-a-store boutique, *Sanger Harris* in Fort Worth, Texas.

Nationally, a surprise! *J.C. Penney* has gone into large-size *fashion* in a big way.

In addition, in pockets across the country, boutiques are opening everywhere. On Fifth Avenue in New York City is a recent import from France, a boutique called *Jeanne Rafal*. Over in Brooklyn is *Charisma's Other Gal*. In Philadelphia, you can find *Plus Woman*, while in Florida, there's *Today's Woman*. San Francisco is home to two large-size boutiques, *Zoftig* and *The Classic Woman*. In Houston there's a marvelous store called *Carroll's*, and in Dallas, *Toy Wynn*. If you chance to land in Toronto, you're missing a treat if you pass by *Liz Porter* and the ultra-elegant *Chez Femme*. Across the country, store chains in large sizes include *Roaman's, Catherine's Stout Shop, The House of Large Sizes* and *Woman's World*. My *unfavorite* is *Lane Bryant*—although, of course, you may beg to differ.

And let's not forget the large-size specialty stores. These were the merchants who always paid attention to our needs, or at least tried to. Even today, they are still in the forefront when it comes to taking a chance whether it's on *fashion* or higher priced merchandise. The department stores still are not 100% convinced that we are willing to spend money on ourselves.

Every week some bright-eyed, enthusiastic and dedicated entrepreneur (who may or may not be a BBW) opens a new, large-size specialty store—dedicated to *fashion*. Be sure to check out each new store that opens in your town. If they're good, give them your support and spread the word. But don't forget your old favorites either. Get used to the joy of shopping in many different stores. We are no longer captive customers of one store. Each store will try harder to get our patronage. They, in turn, will put more pressure on their competiton—other specialty stores as well as local department stores—who in turn will put pressure on the manufacturers. Who ends up the winner? We all do!

Where do you start if none of these is in your area? Start by letting your fingers do the walking through the yellow pages. Phone first. Make sure the places you plan to hit carry large sizes. Go through the yellow pages to make a list of specialty stores for large-size women. If you need assistance, call the yellow pages' business office directly, not the operator. Fortunately, more and more stores are opening all the time. Look at the ads in the yellow pages, since stores with general names such as "The Lovely Lady Boutique" don't quite reveal their specialty, and then call.

If you see a large-size woman on the street who knocks your socks off with her style, go right up to her and find out where she shops.

When you arrive at a store, don't be rushed or apologetic about your size. Shopping need not be the trauma it once was, but it still is far from as pleasant as it should be. You're likely to get angry, but that's normal, and you do have some recourse. When you are harassed in any way while shopping because of your size, please use *BBW Magazine's* "Mad As Hell" coupon to appraise us of the situation.

I'M MAD AS HELL!
I'M MAD AS HELL!
I'M MAD AS HELL!

BBW suggests that if and when you are dissatisfied with the style or quality of the merchandise in any store...or: if you feel that you have not been treated with dignity and courtesy...REMEMBER...You are the customer. Your patronage gives you the right to COMPLAIN. Tear out these slips. Duplicate them. Use Them.

BBW/BIG BEAUTIFUL WOMAN MAGAZINE
5535 Balboa Boulevard, Suite 214
Encino, California 91316

COMPLAINT SLIP

Store Name_____

I have been a customer of this store for _____ years. I am dissatisfied with _____

_____

_____

_____

If you do not make an effort to correct this I will take my patronage elsewhere! I feel I am entitled

to an answer. Please contact me at:

_____   Yours truly,
ADDRESS

_____   _____
CITY   STATE   ZIP   SIGNATURE

BBW/BIG BEAUTIFUL WOMAN MAGAZINE
5535 Balboa Boulevard, Suite 214
Encino, California 91316

I gave a complaint slip to_____
                                    Store name

My complaint was _____

_____

_____

ADDRESS
CITY   STATE   ZIP   SIGNATURE

Give this part to store owner or manager

Mail this part to BBW Magazine

147

GLITZKRIEG

While big women do not yet have a lot of glitzy "name" designers catering to our needs, we have recently been graced by the likes of Pierre Cardin, Gloria Vanderbilt, Halston, Sasson and Givenchy. For the most part, these names entered the large-size market very timidly—lending their names to "safe" items such as jeans and tops with a smattering of traditional (albeit, better-made) pants and skirts. Pierre Cardin, however, has just come out with a *haute couture* line for large sizes.

Manufacturers of better merchandise are still finding buyers for the department stores don't have nearly enough fine merchandise to surround this more expensive stock. Many department stores still straddle the fashion fence when it comes to large sizes. They are afraid to go full tilt into better fashion and let go of what they feel is sure, safe and tested—lower priced polyester tried and true "fat lady" clothes. The problem is just like "real" life: You've got to take a stand. The stores are finding that the less costly polyester merchandise stands out like a sore thumb on racks next to quality fabrics. As a result, they will also find racks of their 'dumb-dumb' clothes remaining unsold. They will perhaps have turned-off potential customers for their better merchandise. Let's face it. Seeing a pure silk blouse for $120 next to a polyester blouse for $29 is a turn-off. Enough said—Let the retail store buyers beware.

FILLING THE GAP

BBW Magazine is very personal. When our readers write, they do not say, "I enjoyed *your* magazine," but rather, "I enjoyed *our* magazine. They look to *BBW* to be their forum and to champion causes which affect BBWs. We, of course, take this honor very seriously.

BBW Magazine welcomed the arrival of designer jeans for large sizes with names on back pockets, particularly Gloria Vanderbilt, since we felt our bigger pockets were perfect for displaying a longer name! But after a while it occured to us that you can only have so many designer jeans at $45 a pair in your wardrobe. Who wants to weed the garden, wash the kitchen floor or deflea the dog in designer jeans?

We felt that while "name" jeans supplied us with fun and style, we also needed less expensive jeans that fit fabulously. Most lesser-priced jeans which fit one place also gave us 'fits' elsewhere.

To fill this gap, we put out a line of *BBW Jeans*. Later we added *BBW*

BBW Jeans

BBW Tops

BBW Tops & Jeans

152

BBW expressly for J. C. Penney

Tops for the same reason. The market had lots of blousy big tops, but not enough "real people" type jean tops. Our *BBW* jeans and tops are found now in most major stores and specialty stores. But, because we feel fashion should be within everyone's reach, and taking into consideration that half of all big women work, we also collaborated with *J.C. Penney* to design a line of fashions labeled *BBW exclusively for J.C. Penney*, found only in those chain stores. We're about to launch a higher-priced line of separates, bras and large-size, junior apparel under our regular *BBW* label, to be found nationwide in specialty stores and department stores.

DOING AS THE ROMANS DO

Shopping outside the USA can be a trauma-filled experience. If you've ever lost your luggage someplace between Kennedy Airport and your destination in Europe, I'm sure you know what I mean. Whether it's in Paris, Rome, Madrid or Lisbon, for the most part, it's the same. You walk into a store and the clerks say, "We don't have anything to fit you here." It's shocking—not only because there are no clothes to fit BBWs, but because the help many times is so blatantly rude. Clerks will look you straight in the eye before you say a word and tell you "We don't have your size here."

After a while, you pretend you don't speak the native language even if you're fluent.

However, in Europe you can find wonderful bargains in flea markets and those incredible tailor shops where beautiful trousers and jackets still can be had. The workmanship is fine and made for the big woman with disposable income—money that the world's chic designers don't seem to want.

Some department stores also carry merchandise for large-size women. Here we've compiled a list for you to take with you on your next vacation. It may save you considerable aggravation.

The stores listed below are taken from the "Shopping in Foreign Countries" section of the *Shopping Guide for Large-Size Clothes* by Elizabeth Cameron. Additional suggestions for shopping for large-size fashions abroad are provided in the guide, which also contains lists of large-size clothing stores in the United States and mail-order lists.*

CANADA

Montreal
  Boutique Anne-Marie
    937 St. Zotique, E. 277-5109
  Pennington's Large Size Shops
    Place Ville Marie 866-6741
    Alexis Nihon Plaza 935-0712
    Carrefour Laval 687-1959
    Centre Laval Ctr 688-8459
    Dorval Shopping Ctr 631-4001
    7915 les Galeries d'Anjou 353-5350
    Place Vertu 334-7135
  Croteau Magasin D'Aubaines Dept. Store
    3930 Ontario, E. 523-2175
  Eaton's Department Store
    677 Sainte Catherine, W.
  Simpson's Department Store
    (downtown) 842-3241

Ottawa

  Boutique Soleil
    1100 Boul Maloney (O. Gatineau) 561-1444
  My Fair Lady
    147 Bank (near Laurier) 232-2056
  Pennington's Large Size Shops
    St. Laurent Ctr 745-9453
    Galeries de Hull (Hull) 770-3916
    Bayshore Shopping Ctr 829-8623
  Eaton's Department Store
    100 Bayshore Dr. 829-9211
  The Bay Department Store
    73 Rideau St. 236-7511
  Ogilvy's Department Store
    126 Rideau St. 236-4511

Quebec

  Pennington's Large Size Shops
    Centred'Achat Place Laurier
      (Sainte Foy) 653-2484
    Place Quebec 523-6885

Syndicat de'Quebec
   405 St. Joseph, E. 529-7351
Eaton's Department Store
   Place Saint Foy (Sainte Foy) 653-9331
Greenberg's Department Store
   90 St. Joseph, E. 529-7722
Le Magasin Metropolitain
   455 St. Joseph, E. 525-4554

FRANCE

In France, stores which specialize in large sizes sometimes use the words "femme forte," or "grande taille" to indicate large or stout sizes.

Paris

   Ambre
      83 Ave. General Leclerc (14e) 327.00.50
   Caroline Femme Forte
      202r Rue Convention (15e) 828.66.67
   Coeur du Sentier
      93 Rue d'Aboukir (2e) 236.75.79 or 236.32.43
   Couturenne Coutriomph de Paris
      80 Rue de Turenne (3e) 272.85.48
   Henriette
      33 Chaussee—d'Antin (9e) 874.25.06
   Mag 2
      131 Rue d'Aboukir (2e) 236.11.18
   Au Printemps Magasin (Department Store)
      64 Blvd. Haussmann, 9e (Most women's clothing is in the Nouveau Magasin building. A welcome room has been established near the entrance from the rue de Provence. Usually there will be someone there who speaks English.)
   Galeries Lafeyette (Department Store)
      30 Blvd. Haussmann, 9e

GERMANY

In Germany the words usually combined with size to indicate large or stout sizes are "stark," "fest" or "dick."

Fussen

Woolworth's
Pedestrian Shopping Street (has large sizes up to size 54 in dresses, slacks, tops, coats)

Munich

Hertie's (Department Store)
Across from the Hauptbahnhof (main train station) (has large sizes up to 56 in skirts, blouses, slacks, jackets, coats; most selection in sizes 50-52)
Kaufhof (Department Store)
Near Hauptbahnhof (has a few items in large sizes but poor selection in sizes over 50)

Frankfurt

Hertie's (Department Store)
90 Zeil Strasse
Horten's
Main-Taunus Zentrum (Shopping Center) Autobahn 66 west of Frankfurt
Kaufhof (Department Store)
116 Zeil Strasse
M. Schneider
Stiftstrasse/98 Zeil Strasse
Peek and Cloppenburg
114 Zeil Strasse

GREAT BRITAIN

London

Buy and Large
4 Holbein Place, SW1
Evan's Outsizes, Ltd.
206 Kensington High St., W8 937-9051
538 Oxford St., W1 499-5372
Manda—The Outsize Shops
57d Kingsland High St., E8 254-8656
Dee Dawson
5 Thayer Street, W1

Sassa
  10A Gees Court
Barker's Department Store
  Kensington High Street, W8
Dickins and Jones Department Store
  Regent St. (between Little Argyle and Great Marlborough Sts.)
Harrod's Department Store
("Figure 18")
  Knightsbridge, SW1
Selfridges Department Store
  Oxford St., W1

ITALY

In Italy the words "taglie forti" sometimes identify large-size women's clothing.

Rome

Releda Mode
  Via Nomentana Nuova, 31/35 (06) 89-05-52
Renascente Department Store
  Piazza Fiume (has a special section on the third floor for large-size clothes, called "Taglie Forti")
  Branches: Milan, Genoa, Naples, Ravenna, Torino, Cagliari, Catania

SWITZERLAND

Zurich

Globus Department Store
  Lowenplatz
Jelmoli Department Store
  1 Seidengasse

*The *Shopping Guide for Large-Size Clothes* is available for $4.95 from Odyssey Enterprises, P.O. Box 1686, Norman, OK 73070.

10 | ACCESSORIES ETCETERA

Clothing is like the canvas upon which an artist paints. You can have the most elegantly tailored suit and marvelous blouse, but the overall picture isn't completed until accessories provide the last important strokes and signature.

Ten thousand women are going to buy that suit you are considering. A slightly smaller percentage will choose a particular style of blouse to wear with that suit. But now that 600 women and you are lined up in the same jade green suit with the navy blue blouse, then what? How do you make it *your* special outfit?

The answer is that it becomes your personal statement by adding your own favorite accessories. The accessories help you personalize your canvas. It's the bit of flourish which tells the world about your style—what it is you wish to project. The language of clothing is universally understood. People react in a different way to you when your appearance says you are domineering, aggressive, shy, retiring, businesslike, on the prowl, awkward, sloppy, chic or standoffish.

CLOTHES MAKE THE WOMAN

For example, if a woman wears that same jade suit with a pearl choker, you get one clearcut image. If another unfastens the top three buttons of her blouse to reveal a gold heart or a zodiac charm, you get

161

quite another vision. The woman with a huge ceramic pie pin with a bite in it is asking for another reaction. A gold pin might indicate wealth and conservative taste.

What are accessories? Thirty years ago they were white gloves, a hat and a single string of pearls (real, near real, or unreal). Add a pair of shoes and a purse (large, small, or extremes of either one), and you were accessorized.

ANYTHING GOES

In today's world of accessories, everything is acceptable. The range goes from prim to punk. We may pierce our ears or our nose for adornment. Telephone cords become pop art belts. The local thrift shop is as trendy as Saks Fifth Avenue. The clip pins and broaches your mom forgot to donate to the church bazaar are cherished now by those who are 'in.' A pin that changes colors, a rainbow scarf, a magnolia blossom in your hair, a colored handkerchief floating out of your pocket for no reason other than you like the color and the effect: *Voila!* Accessories!

My daughter Victoria, who is a professional singer, wears quite a different costume onstage than the one I did in my youth. Instead of a tight, sequined strapless gown with three-inch spiked, pointy-toed shoes dyed to match, plus rhinestone earrings and choker, she favors a splendid, expensively-tailored tuxedo pant suit—with which she wears white satin *sneakers*. And wonder of wonders!—It works!

That's what accessories are all about. They should be fun, and of course, they should accomplish the intended effect. Of course, you have to draw the line somewhere with accessories. I don't think Steve Martin's arrow through the head will get you a prime table at Sardi's.

Still, it takes courage and creativity to go beyond the run-of-the-mill look and immerse yourself in the world of scarves, pins, necklaces, bracelets, rings, earrings, fancy combs, barrettes, ribbons and handkerchiefs. It gets easier once you start paying attention to whatever it is that makes you recognize another woman as sharp and attractive. You must train yourself to look past the face, the figure, and even the basic color of an attractive lady's outfit. Instead, move your eyes to her hair, ears, neck, pocket and wrist. Keep your eye out for added color used either for harmony or for contrast. Soon you will get ideas about what consistently is attractive to you, and then you can try these things out for yourself.

What you do to accessorize a suit reveals your look.

163

SCARVES

Even accessories that are required by certain professions achieve new and unique looks in the hands of tasteful dressers. I am enthralled, for example, with the umpteen ways that stewardesses use their scarves. Although they all wear the same uniform, they are encouraged to personalize it with their scarves. For free advice on the inventive art of scarf tying, you can write directly to the public relations office of your favorite airline or to Echo Scarfs, 10 East 40th Street, New York, NY 10016.

SUNGLASSES

Sunglasses have more uses than just shielding you from the sun. Naturally, you can place them over your eyes and that gives your face a particular look. Drawing them down over the bridge of your nose gives quite another. Your face takes on another dimension when you wear 'shades' in your hair like a tiara or a headband. Or, if you dare, stick the darn things enticingly down the front of your blouse. Take advantage of the fact that nobody has better cleavage to show off than we do. After all, our size seven friends are stuffing to get what we have for free.

DON'T WAIST YOUR WAISTLINE

When it comes to fashion, accessories give you a lot of freedom to roam and experiment. Don't think that because you bought a dress with a belt that you've signed a contract that you must wear *that* belt with it. If you want to go out to a fabric store and buy a curtain tie (they come braided in *wonderful* colors and you can have them cut any length!), who is going to stop you? If you buy a jacket dress with a belt, what law says you can't put the belt around the *outside* of the jacket for a whole new effect?

GIVE YOURSELF A BELT

OK, now let's face this topic squarely. We're talking belts here. Belts for big women. Up to now I've mentioned belts in passing. Now

Sunglasses are a nifty accessory.

Typical jacket-dress.

166

Try belting the jacket for a different look.

I will say it in capital letters: BELTS DO NOT MAKE YOU LOOK FATTER OR THINNER. THEY JUST MAKE YOU LOOK NEAT . . . AND SHARP . . . AND TOGETHER.

Many women are convinced that girdles give you a better line and make you look thinner. Not so. I say that anything you push in from one place is sure to pop out from another. That goes for your body. For the most part girdles succeed in giving you an artificial looking shape. (Tummies pushed in by girdles tend to pop out under our chest or down around our thighs. But they do not disappear.)

When you wear a belt, however, that does give you a better line because it seems to make you want to stand straighter and taller. Of this I am sure. It hurts a whole lot less than a girdle!

What sort of belts should a big woman wear? Any sort of belt she likes which can be found in her size. Wide belts, thin belts, gold belts, leather belts, belts with big buckles, small buckles and no buckles.

If you are not entirely convinced or do not feel brave enough to tuck your blouse inside your pants or skirt, take your favorite tunic top and belt it loosely with a tie belt of matching or contrasting color. You will suddenly change that tired old style to something new.

CHECK OUT THE CHIC BOUTIQUE

Check out all the fashion magazines to spark your imagination. Even old ones in the library are fine. If you don't feel confident enough to accessorize a particular outfit, put it on and head for the trendiest or classiest boutique in town. The salespeople in these emporiums are usually very tuned-in to the particular styles of their clientele and are quite helpful and knowledgeable with their suggestions.

JEWELRY

The one nice thing about accessories for big women is that we don't find ourselves in the same no *woman's* land we do when shopping for clothes. Accessories, for the most part, are a "one size fits all" proposition—except in the case of bangle bracelets where we can't get the darn things over our big beautiful hands and wrists. (Is some manufacturer listening out there?) Oh, for the comeback of Victorian jewelry, especially proportioned to fit the big beautiful woman's dimensions!

Think BIG when you think jewelry

I personally am committed to large pieces of jewelry, and that statement includes diamonds as well. (Again, is anyone listening?) Unless you are absolutely in love with a smaller piece of jewelry, I think proportion should play a part in your consideration. By this I mean that an itsy bitsy ring or charm might get lost on a big woman. There's only one way to find out which looks best on you, however, and that's to try on a large, luxurious piece for comparison's sake.

One good thing about large pieces is that they are at Gucci, Tiffany, Cartier, Bloomingdale's and other quality shops which won't put down your size in the accessory section. Even if a certain store doesn't carry a single blouse in your size, you can find accessories to your taste and preference. Diamond-studded earrings do not need tailor-made alterations.

And by the way, if you *are* one of the fortunate who can afford to drop a few hundred or thousand in purchases, why not take the opportunity to stand up for all large women by expressing your disappointment over the store's lack of *fashion* selection for big women? When your disapproval is followed by handing over a large sum for accessories, the store manager won't ignore you.

If you're climbing up that ladder of success, you want to make sure that you look the part. Think about saving a little bit from each paycheck to buy the kind of accessories that spell success to you: a beautiful leather purse and possibly a briefcase, a status watch (casually elegant which whispers "I'm in the know" instead of "Notice me!"), real gold jewelry—earrings, bracelet and/or neck charm.

CHEAP CHIC

If you are not as financially secure, don't despair—there's plenty of inexpensive ways you can look smashing. Pick up the excellent book, *Cheap Chic*, by Carol Troy, which shows you thousands of ways to make use of thrift stores, other people's attic accumulations and goodies not originally intended by their manufacturers to be used as chic accessories (but they *work*!). For little or no money you can attract as many positive comments as if you had raided a Madison Avenue boutique.

ODDS AND ENDS

The simple truth is that an accessory can be anything not part of the original outfit with which you started out. Atop your head alone you can wear hats (serious, sensuous, suave or so silly), combs, barrettes, tiaras and any number of hair accessories as spices to turn you into a carefully prepared dish. Even a hair style itself—Bo Derek's cornrow braids come quickly to mind—can be more an accessory than a style. We've spoken elsewhere in this book about belts and how they're not simply a prop for the thin. Worn atop an outfit or underneath, they are another aid to good looks you'll want to cultivate.

SHOES

Remember when wearing a tuxedo with sneakers used to be a joke? Now, as I said, my daughter Victoria has convinced me this is legitimate (How *could* you, Vickie?). And remember when Woody Allen wore his athletic shoes with a tux while escorting then-First Lady Betty Ford to a prim-'n-proper Washingtonian affair?

However, I'm still convinced that you can fatally ruin the most-thoughtout outfit and accessories by wearing the wrong shoes. Your attempt at fashion effect from the ankles up is negated if your shoes are soiled, run-down or in any sort of disrepair.

Good shoes, of course, are expensive, but they are vital to your total look. If I could afford only one pair of shoes (though I hope you can afford dozens), I would buy a real leather pump or slingback shoe with a shaped 2½ - 3 inch heel in a neutral color with personality, such as camel. Afterwards, I would take excellent care of them—polishing them and keeping them well-heeled.

Unfortunately, although shoes are another important item, contrary to what some manufacturers seem to think, big, wide feet do not necessarily go foot in hand with large-size women. If your feet are super wide, narrow, very small or very large, you're going to have a helluva time finding shoes that *fit* well, let alone look right. This goes for your size six friend as well as you.

LEG APPAREL

Pantihose or stockings are important accessories, but let me say here and now that I *detest* pantihose. I think the man who invented pantihose absolutely despised women. I have never seen a woman of

171

any age or size—even a model—climb into pantihose with any degree of dignity or grace. I don't even let my husband see me do that number.

It's a shame that pantihose is so predominant today. There is something very, very sensual about getting into a pair of stockings. It loses a helluva lot in the translation when you contort into pantihose.

Even worse, until recently no one ever made pantihose in our size. As a result, most of us walked around at half-mast because we couldn't get them past the midpoint of our thighs! Fortunately, some manufacturers *do* make pantihose with us in mind. A few of the better brands are L'eggs, Room at the Top, Big Mama and Berkshire.

So far as style is concerned, sometimes the monochromatic look is in (e.g., blue stockings with blue outifts), and some favor the very opposite effect, teaming very pale hose with a dark outfit.

LINGERIE AND INTIMATE APPAREL

There are certain undercover things which I also consider accessories—except of course when someone daring decides to wear a piece of seductive lingerie for a night on the town.

One thing for certain about accessories for romance is that your most seductive item is *not* the bathrobe with the hole under the arm. That garment most likely will not lead to a night of mad passion. In fact, it hardly qualifies for shared company over a midnight ham'n cheese sandwich.

If you're trying to get his attention away from Monday Night Football, try a peignoir which fits you well, accentuates your roundness and womanly attributes. Unless your man is hopelessly hooked, you'll soon have him abandoning Howard Cosell for you.

As with tattered bathrobes, the same thing goes for underwear with moth holes in the crotch. The most expensive dress will feel like the frumpiest item on your rack without the right undergarments. We don't want any gray bras which haven't been white since Rosemarie was billed as Baby Rosemarie.

A POCKETBOOK FULL OF DREAMS

You've just bought a brand new outfit—you've accessorized it and even bought new shoes. Your makeup is flawless, and your hair is a vision. You've spent a small fortune wisely but well except for one little thing.

173

Throw away the purse with the broken handle and worn out clasp. Aren't you tired of searching for your house keys for ten minutes until you finally discover they went through the hole in the lining and are wedged into the left hand corner—*again?*

Please don't pull up lame in the stretch. Go the whole way. Remember, you're worth it!

THE LAST STRETCH

Let me close with just a few words about the benefits of good posture. First of all, I'd like you to remember the old adage about the best things in life. Then, as now, they are free. If you don't have the money to buy that velvet belt, or that terrific scarf, or that lovely necklace, the one important accessory you still can have is good posture.

So stand up straight, throw your shoulders back, and look the world square in the eye. Don't be afraid to take up space. You have a perfect right to it.

Remember just how important your body language is when it comes to communicating how you feel. A slouch doesn't make you look smaller; a slouch makes you look defeated.

How can you help yourself? Well, first of all you might try standing in front of a full-length mirror. I'm not telling you to hold in your stomach, either. What does your body language say to you about yourself? Are you making yourself smaller so that no one will notice you? If you are, you certainly aren't succeeding in doing anything but winning the next Quasimodo look-alike contest.

And more than good looks, it's downright unhealthy to slouch. Bend over backwards to help someone, by all means, but otherwise, keep that spine at attention. If you want your back working with you, not against you, it is important you straighten up your act. If you've already hurt your back due to bad posture, you are in very good (or is it bad?) company. Nineteen million Americans visited their physicians last year to complain about back trouble.

And here's another bulletin. Not only is good posture important, but so is good mental health if you want to free yourself from the agonies of nagging back pain. Worry—including worry about weight—may just be the biggest cause of backaches, according to many medical experts.

And in addition to posture, there is one more freebie accessory that you should keep in mind. It's called a smile, and it's the one blessed thing we have where one size fits all. As Karl Malden so often says in his American Express commercials: "Don't leave home without it!"

11	# PARLOR GAMES: AVOIDING THE UNKINDEST CUTS

I've always wondered why when God created me he didn't complete the package and give me fat hair too. If I've said it once, I've said it a thousand times: I'd give $100 for the *right* hairdo. Hair always has been my nemesis. Mine is very thin, finespun and babylike.

UNEASY LIES MY CROWN

My hair has proven a distinct liability whenever I've appeared under the style-destroying lights of television. This was as true during my days as an entertainer as today whenever I represent *BBW* on various TV shows.

God help me if I ever have to appear on a two-hour television special. The curl in my hair works just like clockwork. One hour and "Blip!"—down it goes.

I finally found a beautician who said he could give me "just the right hairdo" for $100.

"Will it stay up for several hours?" I asked incredulously. He assured me that it would.

"Will it make me look like my hair is thick and full of life?" Absolutely.

"Why, this is perfectly marvelous!" I squealed. "Tell me what this hairdo is called."

The gentleman looked me straight in the eye. "It's called a *wig*, Madam."

YOU CAN'T WIN 'EM ALL

In my search for the ultimate hairstyle I have come up with a few styles that I've found pleasing—but like any other woman, I've gotten burnt. One time I booked an appointment with a very chic beautician in New York. He talked, I listened; he talked, I listened. Everything he promised me sounded so wonderful that finally I said, "I'm in your hands." Four hours later, I came out looking like a cross between Mata Hari and Little Bo Beep.

OOH, LA LOCKS

Even Vidal Sassoon, the hairstylist who revolutionized the hair industry 20 years ago, finds it hard to accept the notion there is only one perfect cut for every woman. Because our features change from year to year—and hopefully *we* right along with them—there are many "perfect" cuts for every woman depending upon her current features, age, lifestyle, and working conditions (indoors or out). For example, he says, in the 1980's, women's clothing seems to be more detailed with larger, higher collars. This translates to saying that hair must either be long enough to go below the collar or short enough to stay above it.

I no longer get mortally upset about a haircut or haircolor that doesn't work out. I mean, what's the absolute worst thing that could happen? You could walk out and hate it to death—Right? In a day you can change a wrong color, and in a few months your hair will grow back (with wigs to whisk you past the rough spell). At least you've given yourself the opportunity to be daring, and now it's out of your system. Until the next style appointment, anyway.

When you take a chance, there is also the possibility that you'll love your choice or that the hairdresser will make a new statement that is the *real* you. Or maybe you'll get a hairdo that you're not sure about when it's finished. Why not wear it for a day? You might just grow into it. Like the man who shaves off a long cultivated beard or mustache, it takes us a while to get used to our appearance if it has been radically altered. If it turns out that the style just isn't you at all, it still isn't the end of the world. You'll never *ever* find that special look for you if you don't take a chance sometime.

It's important not to rely on the opinions of others. Whatever they say is just that and only that—an *opinion*. Their opinion is no more true or valid than yours. Should you want some *free* advice, call your 800 toll free operator to get the nearest Clairol or Revlon telephone number. A representative will be most anxious to assist you with questions about haircare.

DYEING FOR A CHANGE

Don't ever let anyone hand you any garbage, no matter *what* their credentials, as to what big women can or can't do with their hair color. There's no law that says you have to be a dirty-blonde or brunette or mouse-colored or somewhere in between—not when there's the magic of all those heavenly colors in a bottle to rely on. Also, no law says you have to be gray. Don't be ashamed to alter your natural state. You are not a fallen woman if you dye your hair.

I found *my* first gray hair when I was 19. By the time I was 26, I was dyeing it. I started off dyeing it maybe once a year, then twice a year, and now I have it done every six weeks because I've turned totally gray but I don't choose to present myself that way. Until I do, I'll wear my hair tinted pink or green or purple or whatever color pleases me. The worst thing that can happen is that you won't like a new color, and you'll have to change it back. Is that a crime? It's far worse to be locked into rigid patterns from which you are too timid to escape. This is why I am not going to offer you advice on specific hair styles for big women. In the first place, what suits a woman in Chicago would not necessarily suit a woman from Hutchinson, Kansas. Everyone is forced to work with the limitations of whatever beautician lives in her area, as well as budgetary considerations. More important, large-size women have as many face shapes as do small-size women. Some of us have round faces, some of us have pointy chins to go along with big or small eyes, pug or aquiline noses, high cheekbones or even *no* cheekbones and so forth.

PLEASE YOURSELF

Look to yourself. As long as it's *your* head, it's *you* a hairstyle must ultimately please. Even if a hairstyle *looks* great on you, it must *feel* great as well. Hairdressers are always trying to frame my cheeks with loose, soft hair which looks good on me, but which I refuse to wear because I cannot stand the feel of hair on my face. Even if the hairdresser succeeded in giving me the finest cut imaginable, I am going to ruin the effect by consciously or unconsciously pushing the hair off my cheeks.

Ignore the well-intended criticisms of those who love and know you. Any time you give someone the opportunity to play God they invariably will do so. They'll offer criticisms they probably wouldn't even have *thought* of making otherwise.

The next time you get a new hairdo and really like it, don't ask your friends or associates how *they* like it. If you must say something, say "This is my new hairdo, and *I* love it." Instead of criticizing, they now will either agree that it's perfect for you or will simply acknowledge that they're glad that you like it.

Many people tend to be threatened by visible changes in those around them. It has nothing to do with the way people feel about you, nor with your weight. Should a *thin*, gorgeous woman suddenly decide to go natural and to strip off all makeup, her friends will be just as threatened as the friends of the ugly duckling who suddenly transforms herself into the glamorous swan.

You can't therefore, worry about what people may or may not think about the *new* you. What do you yourself think? You know what you want to look like. All of us have a mental picture of what reflection we want looking back at us out of the mirror. Of course, common sense dictates that we give ourselves *reasonable* expectations. An Oriental woman with naturally thick straight black hair is wasting her time pining for the carefree abundance of Farrah Fawcett's blonde locks. Even with the marvels of hair bleach the texture of her hair will not do what Farrah's can do. Just as the kid who constantly trips over his own feet should pass on a tightrope walking career.

Take a tip from Popeye: "You am whatchu am!" *Approval starts with you.*

TRICKS OF THE TRADE

Perhaps the most valuable insight I've walked away with from my entertainment career is that appearances are often deceiving. All those people whom we traditionally admire—singers, movie stars and celebrities who are *so* glamorous—are so because they all know tricks of the trade which portray them at their best. There is nothing wrong with that! What's so bad about knowing that if you add a certain eye shadow color it makes your eyes seem bigger?

181

A Ginger Rogers or Jacqueline Smith both have their beauty secrets, and it takes nothing away from their remarkable looks to say so. They're not playing dirty pool with the rest of us by looking terrific. You can do the same thing to accentuate *your* good points. All it takes is a little searching and trial and error to find the right things for you.

Do what the stars do. Take the time—make a conscientious effort to find out what works for you. Allow yourself to appear as attractive as possible. They have given themselves permission to be beautiful (though not necessarily permission to be happy)—and that is every man and woman's right.

So whether you're a movie star or not, it's a good idea to develop a rapport with a beautician, always bearing in mind that you are the buyer and he is the seller. It is far more important for you to be pleased with the product—your hairdo—than for him to impose his will upon you. The minute you leave that shop, his mind is with his next client. Your mind is on your hairstyle, since it is you who must live with it.

SPEAK OUT!

Communicate with the stylist; don't expect to find a hairdresser who doubles as a clairvoyant and can read your mind. Tell him what you desire as clearly as you can. Consider his opinion, but the last word is yours. No one, after all, knows that face of yours better than you do. If you are convinced Bo Derek's braids are what you want, don't let him talk you into a Marty Allen hairdo. You simply tell him: "Look! I want this. If it's no good I'll still pay you for it." In this way you have taken the responsibility for the new style.

Be firm but polite. A simple statement such as, "I've got my heart set on it," works much better than holding a pair of shears an inch from the operator's jugular. Thank him for his suggestion, but insist that you have an itch that won't go away until it's scratched. Filter your response in the way that best suits your personality, but the bottom line is that you as the consumer must get what you're paying for.

Vidal Sassoon recommends that "when establishing rapport with a beautician, first impressions are important and form the foundation for the future." He believes it is important to establish eye contact immediately and to verbalize your confidence in the beautician. "I have full confidence in you, and you come highly recommended," says Sassoon, is the best way to start a positive relationship with a professional.

Wigs can change your own look (above) a little or a lot.

FLIP A WIG OR TWO

Visit a local wig shop to take a sneak preview of yourself in a new hairstyle or color. If you're considering a total makeover, why not try on every darn wig in the store? You're not putting out the sales clerk; after all, she's there all day whether you try on wigs or not. If she proves to be especially helpful, you can always tip her.

The wig store offers you the *perfect* setting to dare and be daring. The absolute worst thing that will happen is that you'll look like Broom Hilda on a bad day. Is that so bad? How long does it take to yank off a wig anyway?

And what if you like how you look? What if, just maybe, you've discovered the perfect *you* that's been kept hidden all these years? Then you can either buy the wig or you can traipse down to the hairdresser's to duplicate the effect with your real hair. Now you have a point of reference when you're talking to the hairdresser. Knowing in advance that you'll like what you're going to get, you'll speak with authority and confidence.

KEEP AN OPEN EAR

But what if you're in the beauty shop for a change, just for change's sake, and you don't have a clear idea of what you want? Why not allow the professional to do *his* job by suggesting something new to you? If you don't like the result, what's the worst that can happen? Aha!—You're learning. You'll hate it and change it—Period. It's not as irrevocable a decision as tattooing the word, "Weight Watcher" on your left forearm.

If something goes wrong and you're not pleased with the style the operator gives you, speak out before leaving. You don't have to rant and curse to get the point across that you are an unhappy consumer. You don't want to back the beautician into a corner where he feels professionably honor-bound to defend himself from attack. Simply state in a kind but firm way that what you've been given wasn't quite what you had in mind. Perhaps he can make a change on the spot, or perhaps you can come back the next day. But don't just summarily say "To heck with him" and never come back. You have no certainty that the next operator will be any more competent than the one you have this time. If the man gave you feelings of warmth as if he were trying to please you, but just didn't quite get it the first time, perhaps you should allow him a second shot. Talk to him again. Work on your communication.

"The future for big women in the hair industry is very, very optimistic," says Vidal Sassoon. "As big women become more aware of their ability to look fashionable, and as they become more comfortable and aggressive in their attitude toward themselves and the image they project to the public, they will definitely have an impact."

One other point to consider in selecting a beauty shop is whether it strikes you as a friendly place. You don't want to patronize a shop where the beauticians give off a "Look who's coming to a beauty parlor!" attitude because you're a larger size than other customers.

WINNING WITHOUT INTIMIDATION

In an unfamiliar beauty parlor all women feel at a disadvantage—no matter what your weight—because of the cliquishness and clannishness of many establishments. There is no need for you to feel additionally out-of-place because of the rudeness of employees. Be yourself, and don't let anyone intimidate you. If, for example, at lunchtime the ladies send out for lunch, don't let the guilty chirping of this dieter or that intimidate you from ordering what you'd really like to eat. We are big people, and we may want to eat a portion larger than a thin person. If we want a hot chocolate with a milkshake chaser, that's no one's business but ours. Forgive me if this seems repetitious, but so much of our conditioned responses to weight came about from an endless repetition of negative images. A beauty shop is a legitimate place of commerce for a big woman. You don't have to be one pound thinner to make yourself up. There are no weight requirements for nifty, up-to-date makeup or hairstyles. The time is now. *You need no one's permission but your own.*

MAKE UP TO YOURSELF

"You have such a pretty face." We've all heard it too many times when it ended with, "if you could only lose weight." It is the ultimate in left-handed compliments.

Now I'm going to say it—"You *have* such a pretty face" . . . period! And what's more, that pretty face will stay pretty for many years *because* of your weight. I always say I have an "inside face lift." Weight keeps my face up and skin smooth and wrinkle free. Put that in your Cheryl Tiegs and smoke it!

So let's talk makeup. One of the rules many of us learned was that big women should use little makeup. The theory was not to be conspicuous and call attention to ourselves, so no one would notice us. What I could never figure out is why you would not want to be noticed. Imagine going through life being the 200 lb. invisible person.

Makeup is not only a useful beauty tool—it's fun too. I have no intention of telling you what color eye shadow you should wear or how to tweeze your eyebrows to give your face a longer look or what shade of lipstick or blusher best suits you. How could I possibly know? One face does not fit all. My suggestion though is to investigate all sorts of makeup and choose what makes you feel the prettiest.

There are a number of ways to experiment. The easiest way is to have a professional makeup done for you. You can find this service in many beauty parlors, you can ask for recommendations from your friends, or you can look through the Yellow Pages under cosmetics. Professional makeups can cost from $15 to $50 and that should include instructions so that you will be able to duplicate the effect at home.

PUT ON A HAPPY FACE

My favorite way to try out new looks is to go to the cosmetic counter in any department store and avail myself of the free makeup by representatives of the various cosmetic companies. They will do a complete makeup for you using their company's products—at no charge. The idea of course is to introduce you to the various products in the hope that you will become a customer. *You are under no obligation to purchase anything*.

If there is a color or item you particularly like, mark it down so you won't forget. But hold off making a purchase for the moment.

Why? Because you have only just begun. Go home and study your new makeup. You may love the entire effect. If so rush back and treat yourself to the whole shebang. It may cost a small fortune, but you're worth it, right? Or you may not like the rouge but you may love the way your eyes look. If so mark down the name and color of the eye shadow, eye-liner and mascara that were used. Also note the name of the company who made the cosmetic, the store's name, and if you can, the name of the person who did your makeup.

On different days go to different stores and get a new makeup. Each time go home and study which portion you really like. Is it the makeup base you like the best? Fine. Make a note. The lipstick? Make a note. Keep at it until you have a fair picture of each of the products and colors you liked the best. Then go back and purchase them. If the person who originally did your makeup is there, ask her to repeat that portion in which you are interested. Bring a pad and pencil with you so you can make a diagram and write down the procedures step by step.

PRACTICE MAKES PERFECT

Then go home and practice. You might not get it right the first time or even the second or third but don't get discouraged. It doesn't take a degree in art to put on makeup—only practice.

I remember when false eye lashes were "in." It took me weeks before I got them to stick in any shape vaguely resembling an eye. At first it always looked like I was wearing a mustache underneath my eyebrows! But in time I learned.

Remember there is no such thing as fat makeup! Each of us have different faces, and we owe it to ourselves to learn how to make those faces sparkle and shine so that it will be noticed that we "have such a pretty face" . . . period!

12 | BIG BEAUTIFUL GIRLS

When I was a counselor in a summer camp, there was a six-year-old girl in my group who was adorable, energetic and bright-eyed. She also was quite chubby. In this camp the custom was for parents to mail in treats which the child was to share with all bunkmates. My chubby girl's mother used to send homemade cookies and candy, but with the expressed understanding that her daughter was not to have any because she was on a diet. In the mornings, however, I would find crumbs all over the little girl's mattress and bits of candy wrappers hidden in her pillowcase. She had gotten up in the dark of night to indulge herself in the same sweets all her friends were allowed to enjoy.

I've often thought of that little girl. She must have considered herself "bad," since good children listen to their mothers. Early on she received the message she was different from her peers in a very negative way. She was big and everyone else was small. In addition, she probably suffered considerable guilt over her clandestine snacking in the dead of night. Can you imagine a child fighting back sleep night after night until everyone else was quiet so that she could find pleasure in a chocolate bar? Her mother had taught this child that she was worth less because her body was *more* than society thought it should be. What crimes have been committed in the name of love!

189

CLASS STRUGGLE

My own hangups about weight go back to my childhood. When I was in the first grade I had a dress which I liked that also happened to be my mother's favorite. Finally, the dress grew tight, but I continued to wear it to school.

One day my teacher called me over. She really liked me and thought she was giving me a helpful bit of advice. "Don't you know you're a little too fat for that dress?" she asked solicitously. I was mortified. How mortified? I didn't wear a dress again until I was 15 years old.

My mother, as I've said before, was bewildered by my feelings about weight. She was always supportive, which helped me through many real and imagined weight crises as a child. I wonder how those little girls whose mothers view weight with disgust and anger make it through to adulthood without becoming raving neurotics. Don't you resent children being manipulated like that? I do.

UNLIKE MOTHER, UNLIKE DAUGHTER

I read a story about a mother whose daughter was 11 years old and a very big girl. The mother was guilty and perplexed. After all, she herself never carried any excess weight. In passing, however, she mentioned that her husband had never been less than 50 lbs. over his "correct" weight all the time she'd known him.

The mother went to a doctor to ask if a tendency toward weight is inherited. His answer was that it was not, and moreover, that it was likely the daughter's size was due to sloppy eating habits.

This mother took a single doctor's advice as gospel. She sentenced her lovely, talented daughter (winner of a statewide spelling bee, a writer of poetry, a whiz at crocheting) to life as a spiritual criminal. This mother thought herself duty-bound to cure her offspring of a terrible affliction. After a year, the woman reports, her daughter is still heavy. This does not deter her. She is bound and determined that her daughter will lose weight—no matter what the emotional torment on the one she loves most.

HEREDITY VS. ENVIRONMENT

If his mother had, in the name of love, done a little more research and a little less harassing, she might have come to the conclusion that her doctor was way off base. If a child has two "normal-weighted" parents, there still is a 10 percent chance that the child will be fat. If, as in this case, one parent is overweight, there is a 40 percent chance that the child will be fat. If both parents are overweight, the child has a better than 80 percent chance of being fat. I really believe that heredity is the key reason why 27,000 diets past and present do not work.

With all the pressure on us and our children to be thin, there still is the fact that approximately 40 percent of the population is considered obese. Isn't it time we say that the rules as we know them aren't right for everyone?

Over and over again we are told: "No one puts food in your mouth and tells you to eat. Don't make any excuses! You're fat because of what you put in your mouth."

But your heritage and background have a *lot* to do with what you put in your mouth. I don't put grits or soul food on my plate because I grew up in an environment that never catered to that taste. If I had been fed those foods as a child, most likely I wouldn't be able to live without those tastes today. Likewise a southern black isn't likely to have ever been blissfully reared on linguini with white clam sauce.

Doesn't it only make sense that a person exposed to heaping plates of pasta every night is going to be heavier than the person whose family serves up raw fish? In this case, ethnic background does play a role in your predilection toward thinness or fatness. Many ethnic cultures too, use the kitchen as the source of social interaction. You get out the coffee pot, huge plates of food and pastries, and you talk all night. There's every chance that a child who grows up in this sort of atmosphere will continue the tradition when he or she grows up to form yet another household.

TAKE MY WORD FOR IT

I sometimes wish I could whisper into the ear of every preteen and teenage girl who is castigating herself (or is being castigated by her loving family), believing her life cannot begin until she loses weight. I want to tell them that there are plenty of size nines out there too who are longing for boyfriends—that there are plenty of girls both thin and fat *with* boyfriends who aren't happy either. When you woo and win it's no guarantee of happiness forever, I want to say to them. Only when you gain peace with yourself by liking yourself whether size three or 30 will you find contentment.

SINGING FOR MY SUPPER

When I was 17 years old I used to play piano in a New Jersey nightclub. While other kids went out on dates I played my music for them. I wasn't working for my bread-and-butter; I was working because what I wanted to do in life was sing, and it was fun as well as perfect training.

One Saturday I was all dressed up in a low-cut dress with rhinestone earrings in my ears and a music book tucked under my arm as I waited for a train to Hoboken, NJ. Seated beside me were several couples quite obviously on their way to have a marvelous time someplace, while I was on my way to work. I suddenly felt so sorry for myself. Like the proverbial little bird whispering in my ear, a sudden thought came to me: "Look to yourself!" *Look to yourself*. I still believe that message was the soundest advice I've ever given myself.

LOOKING TO MYSELF

After all, who forced me to give up dates and spend my weekends banging keys? Who was making me do this? I'm the only one with power over me. It's me that I must blame or thank for all my actions. If I were talking to someone else's little girl, the advice I'd give her is that she must—even at a young age—take control of her life. People *react* to you, but they do not *make* you what you are. Only you can make yourself more or less than you are at this minute.

I'd like to offer ten little suggestions for that darling daughter of yours who thinks she can't be beautiful because she is big. The advice is from one of my *BBW* writers, Joanne Nemes.

GET RID OF HOSTILITY

ONE: You and she must look at her size realistically. You cannot make a big girl small any more than you can make her brown eyes blue. All you will get is scars for the both of you. If she was born roly-poly, chances are that's the way Nature meant her to be. Make it clear that it is her *essential self* you love, no matter what size frame it is wrapped in, and you have gone a long way toward getting her to love herself.

If you yourself are large, don't let any negative feelings you hold against yourself reflect themselves in the way you treat your child. Put your energy into building up a positive image for yourself.

HAPPY MEALS

TWO: Don't fuss over what she eats or doesn't eat. Different families have different eating customs. Some families eat two or three prescribed meals a day without snacking in between. For others, the kitchen is the center of social activity. If you make your daughter stick to a different eating regimen than everyone else in the household, she's going to feel picked on and isolated. Make mealtimes a happy, sociable occasion.

IF SHE DIETS

THREE: If she *chooses* to diet, show your support whether she succeeds on the diet or not. Provide encouragement, but do not police her. Stock up on low-calorie foods and allow her to eat different foods from the rest of the household *if* she assists in the preparation. Don't allow her to eat apart from the family on a regular basis, however. The reason she is dieting is because she feels cut off from a part of humanity; being thin and cut off is certainly not a solution.

TREAT HER RIGHT

FOUR: Don't play the devil's advocate with her. If she is content with her weight as a big beautiful girl, don't deprive her of the treats she craves. Don't reward your skinny son for a good report card with a king-size banana split and then give your large-size daughter a calorie chart as her prize.

TAKE SOME OF THE WEIGHT OFF HER SHOULDERS

FIVE: Keep the same eye out for the rest of the family that you keep on her. Don't tolerate nagging or bullying behavior on the part of her siblings or her father. Stop any derogatory nicknames in the bud, and for God's sake, don't you refer negatively to her weight if you're yelling at her for some *faux pas*. On the other hand, the word "fat" in your four-year-old son's mouth may not have quite the same connotation when he calls his sister a "big fat slob" in anger. If you are overly sensitive to everyday use of such terms, your attitude will hurt your offspring much more than the epithet did, since you are implying that she does, indeed, have something wrong with her. Both you and she must develop perspective.

193

A LITTLE TLC HELPS

SIX: Recognize that you cannot insulate or isolate her from pain caused by the outside world. Your daughter is going to meet some of the same uncaring and unfeeling people that you deal with every day. They are going to attack her size. If she comes to you to air her troubles, soothe her. If she chooses to handle the problem alone, offer your silent understanding. Rushing out with your husband's antique horse halter to whip the neighborhood gang is not going to help your daughter's situation in homeroom the next morning. Your warmth and support at home can go a long way toward mitigating the pain she feels elsewhere.

Teach your daughter that many people are more unthinking than cruel and how to respond forcefully to abuse. Here's a marvelous true story to illustrate this:

Myra, age eight, an adorable strawberry blonde with freckles, came running proudly into the center of the group to show off her new swimsuit. "Hey! Here comes the human beachball!" shouted ten-year-old Tony to make the other kids laugh. Myra stopped abruptly at the edge of the lawn, her lower lip quivering. She turned, ready to run home again, then changed her mind and turned back to face the children. Her face contorted with the effort to keep from crying, but she stood her ground and said: "I want to ask you a question."

The children grew silent. "What am I supposed to do all summer?" she asked. "Stay inside and watch you playing? Can't I have fun, too, or am I too fat for fun?" Tony was astonished and then ashamed. He was clumsy in his little boy attempts at apology, but there was nothing clumsy in the way he took Myra's hand to lead her into the streaming water. By bluntly telling how she felt, Myra put an end to the kind of wisecracks that have hurt all of us over the years.

TEACH YOUR CHILD WELL

SEVEN: Teach your daughter that all of us wrongfully form stereotypes, and then teach her to break any she might possess. Tell her to look for the real people inside the small, thin, hairless, beautiful, heavy—whatever kind of bodies she sees in this world.

INDULGE HER WHIMS

EIGHT: When she is old enough, prepare her for life as a future BBW by spending the time to teach her about fashion, makeup and accessories to enhance her attractiveness. Consider her choices in color, style and fabric. Respond to her tastes and give her the freedom to indulge in her favorites even if they are not necessarily your own. Remember, all girls like fads. If she wants to wear an elastic halter top, help her incorporate the item into a pleasing whole.

DON'T KEEP HER IN A BELL JAR

NINE: Encourage her to be active. Don't push, but if she likes ballet, tennis or track, why shouldn't she participate? See that she has the same outfits that the thinner kids have even if they must be specially ordered. Her clothes should fit her properly. She cannot enjoy herself if they bind, bag or chafe. When she performs or competes, cheer on her efforts. Be there when she wins *and loses*.

KNOW HER SUPERIORS

TEN: Inform yourself about the attitudes of other adults in her life. If teachers, physicians, scout leaders, gym instructors and dance teachers are prejudiced against her size, or are misinformed on the issue of weight, they could harm your daughter. Without being a Meddling Mama, listen to your child as she describes her encounters with these adults, and observe these people as they work with your daughter to see if their beliefs and methods are healthy. If their responses are poor, consult with your daughter about the advisability of pulling her out of their sphere of influence. Changing a teacher at school requires permission of the principal, but don't be intimidated if your child's future is at stake. Insist on a change. You have the right and the power.

The people in your little girl's life should be people who teach through attitude and example that life is good and can be fun. If Mom and Dad are those kind of people, she is off to an excellent start.

13 | THEN COMES MARRIAGE

You've set the date. You're nervous, excited, in love. All the clichés ever uttered apply to you. The world is all aglow. He's handsome, wonderful and yours, all yours. Even your parents like him! Well, tolerate him anyway.

As the day draws near you find yourself involved in a myriad of pleasurable tasks. You work with loving anticipation. Caterers are investigated and evaluated before you finally engage one's services. A deposit is down on a banquet hall, the liquor is ordered, the flowers are selected, and 1001 "must do's" are checked off your list.

TAKEN FOR A BRIDE

Your wedding day is going to be the Big Event you have a right to expect. All that is left is to find the most wonderful wedding gown on the market. You've purchased a stack of bridal magazines and have pored over page after page of white lace, satins, chiffons, and gowns with every conceivable sort of neckline, train and sleeves. In your mind, you have a general idea of how you would like to look on this, the most important day of your life.

Armed with a few carefully selected pictures, you visit your local bridal shop.

After waiting a long turn for a saleslady, your name at last is called. As she approaches, a slight look of—is it annoyance?—crosses her countenance and disappears immediately in a professional smile.

197

NO JOY IN BRIDEVILLE

From here on your joy starts to slide downhill. As you display your carefully cut and pasted magazine pictures, the clerk seems to be murmuring in a preoccupied manner. Why? Because she knows something that you don't. Very few U.S. manufacturers design large-size wedding gowns, and she is wondering whether trying to fit your size 20+ body into a wedding gown is worth her time and trouble. Likely she throws up her hands with an accomplished professional shrug and gives you the business cards of two or three dressmakers.

Frankly, I find the whole business of so-called "ready-to-wear" wedding gowns a bit outrageous. If you detect some heat in my tone it is because I am experiencing mother-of-the-bride traumas at this moment. In my very first visit to a bridal shop I discovered the following truths:

1. Most shops only have sample gowns, and these usually are size ten. This means that everyone who is not a size ten must try to get into the dress as well as possible while straining the imagination to visualize how it will look in the proper size. Never mind the fact that your cleavage is packed awkwardly into the bodice, and that every button or zipper is open so that you can squeeze inside.

2. Wedding gowns are considered "luxury items" and are priced accordingly. Thank God, as we all know, no poor people ever tie the knot.

3. The wedding gown industry's definition of "ready-to-wear" means ready for a better fitting in three to five months. Ask the bridal business why gowns must differ from any other item of clothing. I'm at a loss for the reason.

My daughter Lori happens to be a size five, which puts her into the "grab-a-handful-of-material" class. Trying on the sample gowns, she looks like a ragamuffin or a child trying on Mommy's clothing. I find this sad. At the very least I want her to be treated as a young woman of dignity and grace about to be married.

JUST IMAGINE

It hurts me as well when I see a large-size young woman unable to slip into a size ten dress who is then instructed to "Hold the gown in front of you, dearie." After complying reluctantly, she then must imagine how the dress will look on her. If it were me, this would take an imagination like Einstein's. I want to leave these clerks a blank check as a deposit and ask them to imagine what total will appear when it's finally filled out.

In addition to the indignities I've expressed, large-size women also have a horribly paltry selection. Those hours poring over bridal magazines are wasted, dearie. You'd think that at least one feature or column would mull over the inadequacies of apparel for large-size brides, but they don't. They're the experts; why couldn't they have at least warned you?

They still hold the same perverted belief that much of the fashion industry possessed until recently. In their minds, fat is ugly.

And since fat is ugly, "everyone knows" fat girls don't date. Since they don't go out, they don't have boyfriends or lovers. Girls without boyfriends DON'T GET MARRIED. Girls who don't get married have little need for a wedding gown. The one or two fat women who do get married can choose the easiest solution. Let them don a big, baggy, white mumu, or wrap themselves in a sheet—as Candy Jones, a former high fashion model turned talk-show host, said to me on her New York radio program. *Yes*, she was serious. *Yes*, I was outraged. *Yes*, I let her know it—on the air.

GO FOR YOUR DREAM

In the face of so little selection and so many problems, many BBB's (Big Beautiful Brides) forsake their dreams of a formal wedding and settle for 'something simple.'

If your heart longs to walk down the aisle in a beautiful, traditional wedding gown, to be greeted by your handsome groom attired in a tuxedo with all the trimmings—while your bridesmaids and their escorts (also dressed to the nines) watch from the side—*GO FOR IT!* If it's a little more trouble than your size eight sister had—so be it— maybe it will be easier for *your* daughter.

CLEARING THE BRIDAL PATH

First check out the bridal specialty stores in your area. To save yourself time and the possibility of disappointment, do this by phone. Ask if they can arrange for a bridal gown in sizes 18½ or larger.

You will still have to try on a size ten—but you will be ordering your *real* size. DO NOT let the salesperson talk you into altering a *regular-*

size gown (one that goes up to a size 18 or 20), if you are a size 22. You will *very* rarely be satisfied with those alterations. I've heard too many horror stories about BB Brides being informed one or two weeks before their wedding, that the store was unable to alter the gown. Please, please make sure the gown is being ordered from someone who makes *large sizes*.

At this writing, the only company I know making not only large-size bridal gowns but large-size, maid-of-honor gowns as well is Alfred Angelo Gowns, 601 Davisville Road, Willow Grove, PA 19090. The great part is that they also make regular-size gowns so you can fit your whole bridal party.

Most bridal shops carry Alfred Angelo in regular sizes. They may or may not know he makes large sizes. Ask them to call the manufacturer and check it out.

DRESSES EVEN A MOTHER CAN'T LOVE

If you're the Mother of the bride and a large-size woman, you have your job cut out for you as well.

I could not find a dress I wanted to wear for my daughter's wedding. Anything in the large-size department looked exactly like some smart aleck's vision of *Mama*. On top of that, as I mentioned before, most dresses come in half-sizes which wouldn't fit me anyway. I ended up wearing beautiful, georgette separates. The point is—where there's a will there's a way.

As a last resort, there is always a dressmaker. When you think about what a wedding costs today (I prefer not to think about it), the added cost of a custom-made or custom-designed dress is just one more (gulp!) expense for that most enchanted day.

If you are hesitant about having a full-scale wedding, here are some letters that may encourage you.

> *BBW:* Your fashion section "Rites of Spring" showed wedding gowns for BBWs and I thought I would share with you how *BBW* helped me with my wedding. I have always been big. Not only big but short (5'2", 258 lbs.). In high school I was made fun of and laughed at. I was desperately unhappy and lonely. I very seldom dated.
> Then I met a wonderful man. I was self-conscious of my big body and was almost afraid to have fun. But he was so nice and loving that I started to relax. After our 12th date, he asked me to marry him. I liked him, a lot, but I didn't love

him and I didn't want to fall into the "I'd better marry him because I may never be asked again" trap.

I told him this and he understood but didn't give up. At least once a month he would ask me to marry him. I couldn't understand why he would want to marry a fat woman and so I asked him. He told me that he loved me and that my being big had nothing to do with the person I am and that I am a warm, loving beautiful woman and he wanted to spend the rest of his life with me. He also said that most men like a little extra meat on a woman's bones because they want someone warm and loving to hold on to.

I did some deep thinking after that and realized I had blocked off, in my mind, the idea that any man could love me because I was fat. Our society had planted in me the belief that big women do not fall in love and marry. They just become aunts and nice old ladies. But here was a man who not only liked big women but wanted to marry one. After that I relaxed and let things happen. And they did! I realized that, not only did I love him, but I had loved him for a long time.

Two weeks before our wedding I went to visit my sister, who is also a BBW, and found a copy of your magazine. I read it front to back and felt good. I decided that from that day on I would NOT be called "fatso," "hippo hips" or a "fat slob." I also decided that instead of a small wedding with just the family and a plain dress, I was going to 'do it up right.' I wasn't going to be cheated out of a day that all women want to be perfect, just because I was big. I went all the way—white gown and veil. (I was always told a big woman should never wear white. It showed her fat.) I'm so glad I read your magazine. It gave me the courage to face the world on the most important day of my life. I thank you, and my husband thanks you. I only hope that more Big Beautiful Women decide not to let society ruin their wedding day. I'm glad I didn't.

Joan Foltz
Lost City, W.VA.

BBW: Eight months ago, I met the most wonderful man (in a subway station!) who has helped me overcome my lack of confidence and self-consciousness because of my big body.

With his love and attention, he helped me overcome a very bad habit! I would make jokes about my size in front of people. He would say, "There are enough people out there who will say things to hurt you, so you don't need to hurt yourself." Our wedding is St. Valentine's day and I, too, have decided to 'do it up right'—no plain dress or small wedding.

I deserve to live, love and be happy despite my size.

Josephine Baldwin
Brooklyn, NY

So here's to you, Big Beautiful Bride. Your wedding day should be one of the most extra-special days of your life. Don't let anything weigh you down—especially your weight!

P.S. *Tip for the Mother of the Brides:* Even if you *never* cry, be prepared with not only your fancy lace handkerchief, but some emergency tissues as well. I don't consider myself a crier—but I was not prepared for the emotion I felt when I saw my daughter walking down the aisle in her beautiful white wedding gown.

THEN COMES YOU WITH THE BABY CARRIAGE

Twenty-five years ago, if you became pregnant, your doctor probably would tell you, *"Don't gain any weight!"* He might even tell you to diet during the pregnancy. In those days people didn't seem to take into the consideration the weight of the baby, the water weight, and the weight of the uterus itself which together may come to 20 or 35 lbs.

Today it is widely accepted that during a healthy pregnancy most women will (and should) gain up to 25 lbs. I would be extremely skeptical of any obstetrician today who tells you to diet. We've all heard the horror story about the doctor who told his female client she had a tumor, and six months later she had a bouncing baby boy.

One man wrote me to say that his wife's pregnancy nearly made a wreck out of *him.* His wife's doctor had said that because she was "too big," there was an excellent chance his baby would be born deformed. In desperation he and his wife went to another doctor. "Relax," he was told, "everything's going to be fine. Your wife is healthy, and there's every reason to expect your baby will be normal and healthy as well." The second doctor was right, this man wrote. They had a perfectly healthy baby.

And then there are all the doctors who don't want to see a big woman in the first place who are doubly adamant about hating to see a big *pregnant* woman. Maybe that's why it took so long for any manufacturers to come out with maternity fashions with us in mind. Heretofore, we had to buy blouses a couple of sizes too big and then work miracles with pins and thread or else we walked around with shoulder seams that started at our elbows.

As of this writing, Motherhood Maternity shops have just begun to carry large-size maternity clothes. There are also a few mail order companies in this field.

One such company is called MAX. They specialize in quality maternity fashions of natural fibers. Their address is MAX, P.O. Box 27687, Los Angeles, CA 90027.

Another is Renaissance Lady, 24011 Quail Way, El Toro, CA 92630.

Be sure to check out the regular J.C. Penney Mail Order Catalog under Maternity.

I can't tell you that shopping for maternity clothes is any picnic right now.

If you are not in a position to hire a dressmaker to make you what you need, you might consider the barter system. Surely, someone you know can sew. You might offer to exchange some service of yours (baby sit, doctor a sick plant, drive the kids to ballet class, etc.) in exchange for their making at least one terrific maternity outfit for you.

If your baby grows up to be a BBW, hopefully she will be able to march into any maternity department for what she needs!

MAKE SURE YOU'RE IN GOOD HANDS

One thing you can do during pregnancy to give you peace of mind is to find an obstetrician with whom you—and your husband—are comfortable. Make sure it is someone you trust. Someone you can afford. Someone who is accredited at the hospital of your choice. Someone you like.

The point is that you don't need to be bullied by a doctor. If at first your doctor proves unsatisfactory, you must try, try again. You may not be eating for two, but you darn sure better be thinking for *two*. You don't have to stand for insensitivity or incompetence in a physician. It's not only your health, but your baby's that is at stake. Stand up for your rights. Yours and your baby's. Being pregnant should be one of the most special times of your life. Special for you. Special for your husband. He may not be carrying the baby—but he's "pregnant" too.

14 | TRAVELING IS A BIG TRIP

You've reread the travel brochures ten times, and you've made a definite decision. The reservations are booked, and the tickets are tucked away safely in your drawer. The date approaches. You're excited and happy, but there are also butterflies in your stomach. The thought of being on your own in a strange place—no matter how wonderful a place—sends your normally calm disposition into spasms.

Travel offers the unlimited opportunity for you to fend for yourself. Sure it's not always easy, but when did your parents ever tell you that being an adult was supposed to be easy? Away from home you are faced with the task of looking out for *numero uno*, and it's damn rewarding to learn that you do a fair job of taking care of business.

Various episodes while I was traveling float back to me as if I were viewing a newsreel. The time when I captured the eye of a stewardess who was enraptured with a tall, handsome fellow in a three-piece Brooks Brothers suit and with a smile which said, "I'm a woman too, but also a paying customer!" communicated my need for a blanket.

Then there was the time when I firmly but politely declined a maitre d's kind invitation to dine in the midst of some potted plants when I was unaccompanied—The time I backed down an oily hotel desk clerk who had asked for a tip/bribe and then tried dumping me into a subpar room next to an ice machine—The time I obtained an apology from a brusque drugstore manager who wound up being my friend after explaining that his son was undergoing surgery that afternoon—The time in a Denver hotel restaurant I arrived well after the 9 a.m. rush had departed, and despite the fact that only one other person was present, the hostess marched me all the way back to a table I couldn't have squeezed under if I greased myself head-to-toe. Right then and there, I voiced a quiet but firm objection, and from that day forward vowed to always sit where I want to sit when I walk into a place unless they give me a good reason why I can't ("Sorry, ma'am— That seat's soaked in creosote!"). I noticed the food doesn't get any less expensive when they sit me in second-rate areas.

Oh, sure it takes a while to get used to the unpleasantness of a confrontation—no matter how small or how polite. Lots of women— women of all sizes have gotten inferior treatment over the years, because they've been reluctant to open their mouths. I've finally learned that quietly stewing is much worse for the stomach. If someone must be upset, I'd rather it not be me.

THE SCHLOCK STOPS HERE

Somehow in these times, we've come to accept short shrift: We buy a new car that burns out a transmission the first 100 miles, and we bow our heads and mutter that we've bought a lemon. When the television repairman leaves, we're not surprised two hours later when the T.V. goes on the blink. In a restaurant we get a rude or incompetent waiter and still leave a tip. "The hell with him," we cry into our Visa card, "I'll leave him a tip and never come back!"

Travel is expensive. You will *not* "gets what you pays for" these days unless you are prepared to convince a less—and—less caring population that caters to transient customers.

In a firm, albeit ladylike way, you must demand good service. Service providers are there for *your* comfort, convenience and protection—not the other way around.

TIPS ON TIPPING

1. Do not tip unless you receive good service. No one is *entitled* to a tip. The dictionary tells us a tip is "a small money-gift for service performed." It is not loose change thrown to a beggar. Also, do not refrain from tipping generously with money and compliments when someone has afforded superior service. A word to the person's superior is a way of showing gratitude, as well as displeasure.

2. In a restaurant, if you are displeased with service or attitude, you may request service by a different waiter. You may cut down or withhold the tip completely, but you are out of line to call a waiter any vile names.

If you have been unhappy with service, more often than not, the fault may lie partially with you. In a restaurant, the difference between prompt service and "I'll get it when I have a chance" service depends upon the way you request assistance. "Waiter! Would you mind getting me a glass of water, please?" never works so well as "Waiter! A glass of water, please!" Tacking on a smile and thank you with your request is never out of order.

3. Eating cold or undercooked food for which you are required to pay hot and overinflated cash is an exercise in wastefulness. Never accept food you don't like. Send it back—politely—with your reason stated succinctly. Be prepared to say: "I am not happy with the _____; it's too _____. Please bring me _____ instead.

Make your comment a statement, not a question. When you arrived the waiter *took your order*. If the food is not prepared according to your order, you have the right to send it back.

TAXIS CAN BE TAXING

Don't be timid in restaurants or in taxi cabs. A cab driver once tried to do a double shuffle with me when I shared a ride with a lady from the airport in San Diego to our adjacent hotels. He tried to charge *each* of us the fare on the meter even though there were no signs to warn us that this would be the case. In a metered cab, you are required to pay what is on the meter (plus tip), unless you are otherwise advised, beforehand, by word or sign. I refused to pay the driver, inviting him to come into my hotel to call the police to report the incident. Naturally, he declined because what he was doing wasn't cricket. He went away with my half of the fare (minus tip—I don't tip people who try to cheat me). Did I feel proud of myself? You bet your Fig Newton I did!

Don't get me wrong. I love cab drivers. The majority are terrific guys. I've been known to overtip many a kind, warm cabbie on a cold winter's day for rescuing me before I froze to death on the streets of New York.

THERE'S NO PLACE LIKE HOME (SOMEONE ELSE'S)

Even the fact that I'm on the road these days more than off it, I still get a thrill out of experiencing new adventures. "Faraway Places with

209

Strange-Sounding Names" remains a special song that sends a peculiar ache of longing down my spine.

I hope this love of finding a new and exciting world through travel excites you too. So many BBWs, unfortunately, hold off taking a dream trip until they lose weight. What a pity! All these women putting their lives on hold until some new form of Metracal arrives magically to turn them into gorgeous butterflies.

What's worse, is deciding to see Europe and then dieting your way through the finest restaurants on the continent. What a time to diet when you should be enjoying the trip of your life! I mean, if you have to diet at all, why not *diet before you depart?* What's the sense of restricting yourself on a dream vacation?

Other BBWs live their lives to the hilt on vacation. One empties out her suitcase in Europe and comes back with all new clothes. Others take a pair of sneakers and some comfortable jeans, prepared to walk everywhere and experience every wonderful thing they can. These women have put their lives on "full steam ahead."

CHOOSE PACKAGE TOURS WISELY

BBWs may want to avoid package tours emphasizing sun and sex such as the Club Med where the object is to see who can wear the fewest clothes for the longest amount of time. Instead of choosing such shallow-thinking tours, why not gravitate to package tours that have more to offer than flesh contests? If hanging around a pool all day is your idea of a good time, however, there is no reason why you can't do that, too, on a tour that offers additional bonuses besides peek-show mentality.

LET IT FLOW, LET IT FLOW, LET IT FLOW

If you like to ski, hit the Austrian Alps by all means, but if you can't stand the sport, don't bully yourself into staying in a ski lodge all day on the chance you'll meet a super guy with a cast on his leg. You're sentencing yourself to the possibility of a rotten vacation.

Too much tension is involved when you set your sights on the "big romance" instead of meeting men *and* women as a natural extension of the good time you're having. Go out and meet human beings as human beings, male or female. There are lots of unattached souls out there whose company and conviviality you will enjoy. If there's a 'shipboard romance,' like in the movies, fine and dandy. Just don't make it the focal point of your trip.

210

BREAKING OUT THE ICE

A friend of mine named Pam Winger is a *BBW* writer and travel agent who often goes on shipboard cruises. She insists that weight is no deterrent to becoming the life of the ship. If you're enjoying yourself and having fun, other people naturally gravitate toward you. The only thing Pam won't do is get up at 6 a.m. to join the morning fanatics jogging around the ship. She says that all her extra calories are knocked off in the evening, when she's busy disco dancing until 2 a.m.

Once aboard ship, Pam has a guaranteed method for meeting people instantly. The second the ship leaves port she shouts out at a group of passengers: "Hi! I'm Pamela—C'mon into my stateroom and have a bon voyage drink."

She's immediately created a situation where six to eight people are going to ask her later to their rooms for a drink. I defy anyone not to make friends this way. Even for people who've never opened their mouths in their lives, it works like a charm. Once shipmates find out how much fun you are, you're the one they want around them.

How can you get some idea of the cruises and vacations that are right for you? Locate a travel agent you trust who has the time and interest to give you some personal attention. A good agent will make sure your accommodations on planes, boats and so on are satisfactory for a large person. A good travel agent will know that airlines have certain flights with small seats and other flights with comfortable seats aplenty. The accompanying chart will give you some idea what airline seats are best for you.

TUSH TABLE

FLY IN COMFORT ☑ SEAT SIZE CHART
Seat width measurement in inches with arm down

FIRST CLASS	707	727	737	747	DC-8	DC-9	DC-10	L1011
AIR CANADA	—	20	—	20¼	20.9	20	—	20¼
AMERICAN	20.5	20.5	—	21	—	—	21	—
CONTINENTAL	—	21	—	—	—	—	21	—
DELTA	—	17	—	—	18.5	29	—	17
EASTERN	—	20.87	—	—	—	20	—	20.87
EL AL	16-17	—	—	21	—	—	—	—
KLM ROYAL DUTCH	—	—	—	20.5	—		20	
LUFTHANSA	28.3	28.7	28.7	28.3	—	—	28.3	—
NATIONAL	—	21	—	—	—	—	20	—
PAN AMERICAN	22	—	—	21	—	—	21	—
S.A.S.	—	—	—	21	—	—	18	—
SWISSAIR	—	—	—	21	—	—	21	—
T.W.A.	20.9	21	—	21	—	—	—	20.9
WESTERN	19¼	19¼	—	—	—	—	21¾-23¼	—
UNITED	—	21	21	21-22	20-22.5	—	21-22	—
ECONOMY	**707**	**727**	**737**	**747**	**DC-8**	**DC-9**	**DC-10**	**L1011**
AIR CANADA	—	18	—	18	16.5	18	—	18.5
ALITALIA	—	—	—	20	—	—	—	—
ALLEGHENY	—	—	—	—	—	18	—	—
AMERICAN	17	17	—	17.5	—	—	17.5	—
BRANIFF†	—	13	—	—	—	—	—	—
CONTINENTAL	—	17.42-17.66	—	—	—	—	17.42-17.96	—
DELTA†	—	17	—	—	18.5	20	—	15
EASTERN	—	17.25	—	—	—	18.5	—	—
EL AL	16-17	—	—	16.17	—			
KLM ROYAL DUTCH	—	—	—	17-18	—	—	17-18	—
LUFTHANSA	19.6	19.2	19.2	21.6	—	—	19.6	—
NATIONAL	—	17¼	—	—	—	—	17.5	—
PAN AMERICAN	17¼	17¼	—	17⅝	—	—	—	—
P.S.A.†	—	23	—	—	—	—	—	—
S.A.S.	—	—	—	17.5	—	—	17.5	—
SWISSAIR	—	—	—	17.5	—	—	17.5	—
T.W.A.	16.8	16.8	—	17	—	17.9	—	18
WESTERN	16.5-17.5	16.5-17.5	—	—	—	—	17.42-17.96	—
UNITED	—	16.5-17.5	16.5-17.5	18.5	16.5-17.5	—	18.5	—

†Width of underseat

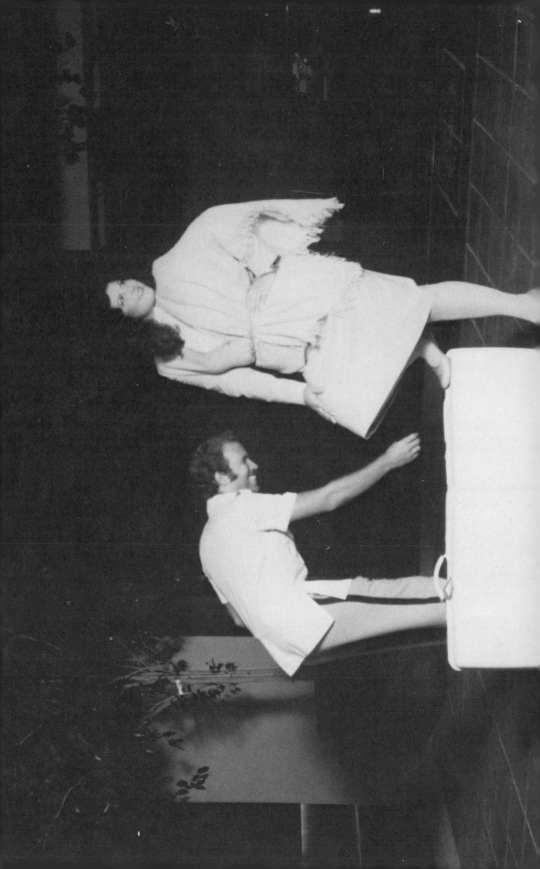

COME FLY WITH ME

Many big people are unaware that seat belt extenders are available for further comfort. Most aisle and window seats in economy are about one-inch smaller than the middle seat. If you should require two seats, CAB regulations require that you pay for only 1½ seats. Should there be an empty seat, ask to be seated next to it and request a refund of the extra half seat. When making reservations, request smoking or non-smoking sections in advance. Get to the airport early, since you're not guaranteed a non-smoking seat after standbys are seated.

Personally, even though I realize the aisle seat is an inch smaller than the middle seat, I always request an outside (aisle) seat. You have more room to stretch your legs and needn't wait until it's almost too late when you have to make a trip to the ladies room. Also, it saves you from becoming prematurely intimate with your traveling partner when you have to clamber over him to get past.

TAKE A LOAD OFF YOUR BACK

The whole idea when traveling is to pamper yourself. When possible, get a porter to carry your bags in or out of the airport. Ending up with a back plaster on your back for the remainder of the trip is certainly not worth the two bucks you'll save by hauling your own luggage.

Airport limousines are an excellent way to get to a major hotel from the airport. However, if your destination is not on a regular limo stop, and you need to transfer your jet-lagged body and four valises from the airport limo to the cab, it may be worth the extra ten dollars to hire your very own cab right from the airport.

Or, if you can afford it in your personal or professional budget, why not hire a private limousine? They range from $26 an hour (two hour minimum) on up depending on the luxury offered. A few even have special airport pick-up rates of $30 to $36 with a 15 percent tip included.

Imagine stepping off a plane in a strange town and having a uniformed gentleman hold up a card with your name printed on it, who will relieve you of your packages and make you comfortable in the limo, while he takes your luggage stubs and fights crowds at the baggage claim. If it sounds too heavenly for words, it's only because it is.

215

ENJOY YOURSELF

If traveling by wheel is more to your liking, use the good-to-yourself method of travel and treat yourself to at least one meal a day in a charming restaurant. Stay in the *nicest* place you can afford. Travel is no time to save money.

If your idea of a swell trip is aboard a mule with a backpack or a husky-drawn sled, go for it! My concern with creature comforts might not be your concern. I don't want to cheat you out of your dreams, so *Bon Voyage*, and wave as you pass me.

Myth:

BIG WOMEN LIKE THEIR FASHIONS EXHIBITED ON SKINNY MODELS.

This Pendelton ad appeared in **Redbook** in 1979. The model is a *size ten*.

This is the same Pendleton suit as it appeared in a fashion layout in *BBW Magazine* in 1979 on a large-size model. Now honestly folks — Who looks better in that suit?

We wish to thank Pendleton, who graciously allowed us to use this ad. We are delighted to inform you that Pendleton now uses large-size models for their Women's sizes.

False.

As I said before. WE GOT FAT. WE DIDN'T GET STUPID! We **can** tell the difference between a size ten and a size 20. You don't see small-size clothes shown on a large-size model. Why should anyone believe that we want to see our fashions on small models? We acknowledge that there are thin people in this world. Isn't it about time that designers, manufacturers and retailers acknowledge our existence too?

15 | SO YOU WANT TO BE IN PICTURES

If you don't try, you'll never know if you can make it.

That may not seem very profound, but it is a truth I pass on to every BBW who asks me if I think she can become a large-size model—or attain any other dream for that matter.

At least today, a large-sized woman has a *chance* to become a model. As late as 1979, where was a 200 lb. woman going to get the opportunity? Anyone who harbored such ambitions was ashamed to say so aloud because people would have laughed. No one over a size six had a prayer of modeling, even if your face was gorgeous enough to send men reeling with twin coronaries. If you walked into a modeling agency, they would have handed you a mop or told you to drop 100 lbs. and *then* go on a diet.

What a difference this new decade makes! Many of your dreams can come true! I know. My dreams have been granted, and I'm overjoyed when other people's most-cherished ambitions are realized.

FOR WHOM THE BELLES TOIL

Different kinds of modeling are open to a BBW. If you're not right for one, you may be just perfect for another. There are very few women who fit the bill of the "ideal" specimen—but who can do it all?

223

Among the many new opportunities that exist are: work as a photographic model, work in fashion shows and fit modeling (acting as a sort-of living mannequin for designers).

Before you grab your pictures and head out toward the nearest boutique, however, think about what you're contemplating. Modeling is not as easy as it sounds. What would you do on a 3 x 12 foot ramp in front of 300 pairs of eyes—all of them focussed squarely on you? Where would you put your hands? How would you walk? What would you say when someone out there throws you a comment? What if you tripped? What if, in your hurry to get on to the ramp, you discovered your bra was unhooked?

ARE YOU PICTURE PERFECT?

I've had gorgeous girls come into the office only to discover that they photographed poorly—a disappointment for both of us. On the other hand, girls who look rather ordinary in person sometimes photograph like living angels. Who can explain why a camera lens loves one woman more than another? Nonetheless, it takes a special gift to have beauty, grace and the ability to look like your body is moving while you're standing still to pose.

RUNWAY WINNERS

Runway modeling in fashion shows demands a special person who is in complete control of her body. You can't be self-conscious about your movements. While a girl who shies away from crowds of people may make it as a photographic model, a runway model needs a flamboyant, extroverted personality. On each job, you are in direct contact with the public, selling yourself and the clothes on your back. Openings for fashion show models of large-size fashions exist at many department stores, boutiques and specialty shops.

I have a model named Helen Lipton who is a corker when it comes to runway modeling. People just *love* her. She's a big woman my age, and when she does a show, she has the time of her life. So does her audience. Helen makes Cher look inhibited when she sashays out to perform.

What makes a successful large-size runway model? The ability to come off as a real human being out there. People must identify with you.

The nice thing about the large-size models I've worked with, is that

Helen Lipton

they are *so* helpful to one another. They lend each other whatever it takes to help them look better. It's not a matter of, "I have the shoes she needs, but I'll be damned rather than let her borrow them and look better than me!" Big models tell one another what looks good as an accessory with this or that outfit. They are always giving one another tips. I hope it continues. Right now we are still a small family.

PEACHY KEEN

Typical of the women I've worked with is 22-year-old Conni Peach. Conni admits that it was frightening when she first decided to pursue a career as a model. But in her three years of professional modeling she has developed the aggressiveness, the stick-to-itiveness and the willingness to work as hard as it takes to succeed. Conni has a photographer's eye for instinctively knowing what will liven up a photo. She doesn't keep a good idea just for her own photos either. "Why don't you try this or that?" she'll call out, and often her suggestions are used.

I find a healthy, vivacious spirit to be true of all large models, no matter what area of the country I travel to for shows. On one memorable occasion, I went to do a show in the small town of Greeley, CO. It was far enough away from Denver that the show's sponsors decided to recruit local models. The women they found were not professionals, of course. None had modeled in their lives. Is there anything greener than green? If so, these women were it. But I had one of the finest times in my life there.

SPIELBOUND

Before the women went on, I gave them the spiel I always give my models, experienced or not. "Now listen," I said, "the most important thing you can do on stage is to have a good time. If you have a good time, the audience will too. What they want to see is a big woman in pretty clothes feeling terrific about herself. I don't want to see anyone imitating a *Vogue* model, looking down your nose at the audience. I want you to be real people out there."

"Another thing you must remember is not to go out and be mesmerized by the lights and the crowd because I'm going to be talking to you. I do a non-stop monologue so that out of the blue I might ask you to whisk off a belt or inquire what you had for lunch today. If you're standing there stone-stiff ignoring me, both of us are going to wind

Conni Peach

up looking pretty silly. Please don't leave me out there with egg on my face!"

Well, I could see it in their eyes. These women wanted to shine out on stage; they really did. If I asked them to jump into the audience and do a two-step, they would have tried without a single objection. Everything went surprisingly well once the show began—until I started to ask the models little questions. Oh, they heard me all right. Their ears were *glued* to the sound of my voice. The problem was that each and every one of them stopped dead still and turned to face *me* while I talked to them, instead of going through the motions of showing off their fashions. I had to keep saying: "No darling, no! Turn around and face *them!*" But you know what?—everyone had a tremendous time because the models were so "human."

COUNTRY GIRLS

Another thing I noticed is how uniquely different the models out in one section of the country are from another section. They are all voluptuous, but they all have their own special looks.

The models in Dallas are absolutely gorgeous. Texas has the blonde, cheerleader types with a look of old-fashioned sexiness. Perhaps they move their bodies differently because they are used to riding horses. They move gracefully, like athletes.

In Seattle I've met some of the most beautiful mature models. They have a confident, glamorous air about them. They're women who have known success in various enterprises and show real class on stage. Some of them own cosmetic businesses; a few are fashion designers. Large-size models come from all walks of life. Some of the nicest mid-American types are in Indianapolis. One Indy woman started a club just to make big women feel good. It's not commercial in any way. She's just a giving person who enjoys communicating with people.

The models in Manhattan have a real New York look. The New York look is a glitzy look. It's more tuned into the interesting face than to all-out beauty. There's a difference; it's more severe. New York models are more sophisticated; they have to be. The models are a little thinner too. Seventh Avenue has not yet learned that a size 14 isn't fat. Still, they are headed in the right direction.

Chicago models, I've found, are a blend of east and west. They are relaxed and as fresh-faced as West Coast models with a subtler veneer than their New York counterparts. It's a charming mixture of wholesomeness and sophistication.

Sherry Staab, Dallas

Mar and Mary Duffy,
New York

San Francisco models are blessed with beauty, sophistication and a kind of excitement and pride that seems to go hand in hand with living in one of America's most breathtaking cities.

In Hawaii I found that both the models and the audience were very warm, very effusive, very touchy-feely people. The models were terrific to work with and tried so, so hard to please. We had audiences of 200-300 people laughing, applauding and yelling like crazy. At the end of one such show the people in the store said to me: "Carole! This never happens! Hawaiians are not a demonstrative people." I guess that being a big beautiful woman sometimes even passes over cultural proclivities.

MODEL CITIZENS

Of course, not everything about modeling is always so pleasant. For weeks at a time a model may be out of work. As a freelancer, more often than not, you are ineligible for unemployment benefits. You also must understand that rejection goes with the territory, just as it does for small models. You can be sure that Cheryl Tiegs was turned down for jobs during her career. Yet each day I get outraged letters from would-be models who are upset because a store or modeling agency pointed thumbs down. I'm sure many girls who have applied to *BBW* hoping to land a fashion spot were disappointed when our fashion coordinator didn't use them. Consequently, it is imperative to believe in yourself despite a certain inevitable amount of rejection. Anyone who takes a turndown as a personal affront every time is not made for this business. You *must* expect rejection and grow stronger in the face of it.

One thing models don't take into consideration is that a fashion show coordinator is looking for specific types of girls for a job. He'll turn down the most gorgeous blonde in the world if a redhead is needed.

Another restriction that many agencies have is a height requirement. Girls usually must be no shorter than 5'7" and no taller than 5'10". The reason is that there isn't time to take up a hem or shorten sleeves for a photo session or a fashion show. A tuck here, a pin there—Maybe! But no extensive alterations are tolerated.

So what about the models that are 5'2" and 5'3"? Eventually we will have petite, large-size models, but it won't happen overnight. Look how long it took the fashion industry—80 years or better—to realize that not all women are size 12.

Joette LaFond

TALL SUCCESS STORIES

BBW uses several six-foot tall models. One is 22-year-old Joette LaFond. Joette insists that modeling isn't as glamorous as it's cracked up to be. There are times that she's appeared in a gorgeous outfit on a roof cluttered with dead pigeons. Often the girls must dress together in a dressing room no bigger than a breadbox, or together with male models in their skivvies.

In addition, Joette must supplement her modeling income. Few models manage to line up enough of those sweet-sounding $125-an-hour appointments to quit their day jobs. *BBW* model Bonnie McClain is an opera singer; Sandra Zagaria was the talent coordinator for the John Davidson Show; others are teachers, university instructors, receptionists, secretaries and housewives. Joette is a checker at a supermarket.

DOLL FACE

Courtenay Leigh is another whose interests span more than modeling. She's done movies, acted on stage, taught high school and is a professional singer. Courtenay was the model for the *BBW* large-size mannequin which is helping to revolutionize the garment industry. Instead of showing our-size fashions on a size eight mannequin—or more recently on a size 14 mannequin—whose faces consciously or subconsciously were not made as pretty as smaller mannequins—we took matters into our own hands (or should I say, bodies). We had a mask made from Courtenay's face for a mannequin with the precise proportions of a size 38 top and 32 bottom. Unfortunately, the first experiments were sent back to the drawing board when a strange thing happened. The mannequin looked too *small*, and we had to make the bottom a 34, since we wanted no mistaking that this was a BIG, BEAUTIFUL MANNEQUIN.

Courtenay is one of my favorite people. She's glib, she's intelligent, and she's in love with what she does. She loves not only the idea of modeling, but also the idea of the emancipation of the large-size woman.

Often it amazes me that a woman of her great beauty and flawless complexion should ever have been hassled by anyone in this world. Right now she's getting lead parts in plays which show off her beauty, but this is only after many years of paying her dues. Although a young woman, she long had to contend with being offered only such parts as the mother, the older woman and the plotting contessa.

232

Saundra Zagaria

Bonnie McClain

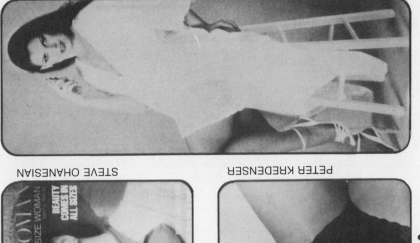

B. Courtenay Leigh

Height: 5'7" / Size: 18
Hair: Auburn / Eyes: Hazel
Pants: 34 / Shoe: 9/10

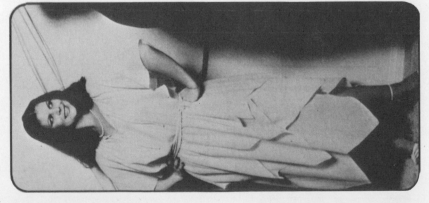

GLORIOUS

Another woman I take special pride watching grow professionally is Gloria Mushonga. Gloria appeared at my office one day without an appointment. Ordinarily, I can't see anyone who just drops in unannounced. Things are just too hectic. When I glanced into the outer office, something about her immediately caught my eye. Three days later I had her on a fashion shoot.

It was rewarding to learn why Gloria came to *BBW* in the first place. As a beautiful black big woman, she says that she is dedicated to the premise that all women like herself can find peace within. Formerly married to a man who kept pressing her to diet, Gloria says that she learned that no one else can carry your weight or make you change it. "I came here to model," Gloria likes to say, "because I really believe in the essential idea for which *BBW Magazine* stands. Just as the blacks and Chicanos have done, big women are accepting themselves and identifying with one another."

Consequently, Gloria has become one of our most popular models, both before the camera and on the runway. One reason is that she and her three sisters used to pose for their father, a commercial artist, for Pepsodent, Toyota and Yamaha advertisements. Later she went on to slim-size modeling before her marriage.

What Gloria emotes on a runway is incredible. Put a Western outfit on her, and she immediately assumes the hipswayin', bowlegged look of a cowgirl. Put her into lingerie, and she'll draw every man in the store away from their size-six girlfriends. All the while, she'll keep up a captivating repartee with the audience. "How ya doing?" I'll ask her when she struts onto the runway. "Great!" Gloria will smile. "I've taken the dog to the vet, the kids to dancing school, and now. . . ," she winks coyly in her best Lena Horne manner, "I'm going to take some time for me."

MAKEUP SESSIONS

Like many small-size models, Gloria and the other girls put on their own makeup and fix their own hair. If you harbor a dream of becoming a large-size model, it would serve you well to acquire these skills. Take a course if you want to or simply learn by doing. You've got to be able to work quickly. There may not be a makeup artist at the fashion show.

I must admit, even after all this time, I still get a tremendous kick out of watching the models put on their makeup. Every model has her

Gloria Mushonga

own tricks, her own way of doing things. Each girl knows her own face so well; they're almost like painters attacking a canvas. It's absolutely enthralling! I can sit there for hours watching—and I do!—while Courtenay puts on nine different shades of eye shadow.

I think this preoccupation with good grooming is a sign of consummate professionalism. The difference between a stunning model and an "ordinary" woman may be the difference between clean, well-cut hair and a merely adequate hairstyle, between good posture and careless posture, between smart cosmetic use and cosmetic abuse.

Models have learned to pamper themselves almost shamelessly. Professional facials and massages on a regular basis, weekly or biweekly trips to the beautician and manicurist, and the upkeep of a clean and sharp wardrobe help a woman think like a model. Once you begin to think like a model, you're already moving out of the starting blocks when your first call comes to be ready for a job that afternoon.

DO I NEED AN AGENT?

Speaking of jobs, I'd like to abolish the notion right now, that outside of New York City a large-size model *must* have an agent if she is to succeed. There are few agencies who handle large-size models exclusively. Many established agencies refuse to have anything to do with large-sizes. Others that will take on a few big girls do not have enough real interest in this new field. As a result, they won't get you any more opportunities than you could get for yourself. Some large-size models are so thrilled to be signed to an agency that they get their *own* jobs and pay commissions to the agencies anyway.

To be honest, the large-size market today is more for fun than profit. It is not ready to support many models full-time. If you're a person who looks great, moves right and gets herself connected, it really is a lot of fun.

Develop the attitude that you can do it on your own, and you can. Begin modestly. Have some simple 35mm snapshots taken of yourself by a friend. Don't spend hundreds of dollars on a portfolio, yet. All you need are good clear shots that show you full-length and in a close-up. Don't submit something that looks as though it's been snapped in a dark alley. If the top of your head is cut off, and it's not clear whether you're blonde, brunette or bald, schedule a second shooting.

GETTING DOWN TO BASICS

On the back of your photos, attach a label listing your height, your dress size (not your weight), your blouse size, pant size and measurements—as well as your name, address, and phone number. Have enough copies made to take around to every department store and large-size specialty store in town. Introduce yourself to the Director of Special Events. Try the print media, including publishers of catalogs which sell large-size fashions, and of course, manufacturers.

Don't worry too much about your lack of experience at this point. The large-size industry is relatively new. Most large-size models have only a few months experience. After all, until some brave girls began getting through the doors they hammered on constantly, *no one* had any experience. Where were they going to get it?

If you decide to model, why not jump in with both feet? Take whatever respectable jobs you can get to build a portfolio with professional shots and published work in particular.

Modeling is like show biz. Sometimes, at first, you work for free. Later perhaps for Coca Colas and carfare home. Once you earn some credits, you can begin to demand money, but you must be *worth* a fee if you expect to be paid.

If you think it's tough now, try to imagine what it was like for large-size models like Idrea, who pioneered the field in the late Seventies. She was beautiful but big, saying: "Here I am—I want to be a model."

THE NOT-SO-GOOD OLD DAYS

Can you even conceive of the reaction she received—from outright scornful laughter to no end of ridicule. *"What are you?—some kind of Nutcake!" "Have you been smokin' something funny, kid?" "Come back when you've left half of your behind, behind."*

Yet Idrea persevered, going back again and again to see these same people until they developed a human relationship with her.

After a considerable lonely time, she was no longer categorized as a fat, crazy girl who wanted to be a model. Her individual personality began shining through. Now her name was attached to her face. She became known as the one who wouldn't quit. Instead of a fat person coming through the door, employers began recognizing a fellow human being. Finally, it had to happen. One courageous soul said to Idrea: "Everyone's going to think I'm crazy, but come on! I'm going to take a chance on you."

IDREA

SIZE: 38/32
HT: 5'6"

HAIR: MED. BLONDE
EYES: GREEN

This was a large-size manufacturer, remember. The rest is history. Public reaction was terrific, and business increased. Slowly but surely, for purely economic reasons, other manufacturers crawled—if not exactly jumped—onto the bandwagon.

At *BBW Magazine*, I am proud to report, every advertiser uses a large-size model for showing clothes or I will not accept the ad. However, since there is no such thing as fat toothpaste or fat hair color or fat perfume, we do accept those ads with small models. Agencies are just beginning to realize that large women will help the client bring in a profit. The laughter is slowly dying down.

If you harbor dreams of becoming a large-size model, be assured, that though the ground is broken, the seed has not taken everywhere. You'll have to be persistent to succeed. Once you drop off your photos, don't expect your phone to ring off the hook. You'll have to do a lot of phone and legwork to impress a potential employer with your zealousness.

If and when you put yourself into the marketplace, don't let any employer or model agency coordinator speak to you in any other way but a polite manner. I've heard many horror stories about women who have taken their heart in their hand, gotten their pictures together, and then left an agency in tears. Agents can be rude ("Don't come back till you lose that wart!") or insulting ("Forget it, Kid—you'll never make it!"). They can demonstrate quite clearly that they are holding back laughter or a nasty comment. Sometimes you won't even get to the agent: the receptionist will destroy your confidence with her attitude. If it is within your capabilities, you must put such people in their place.

FUN FOR ALL

Should everything come together, including a helluva lot of luck, there are many, many perks that you enjoy as a model. First of all, there is the wonderful feeling of being wanted. Then there's the glamour. Getting fussed over by a makeup artist and hairdresser is an incredible luxury. Every time you parade in front of an audience or watch someone examining your picture in *BBW Magazine* or some catalog, you get warm feelings inside. These women are vicariously sharing your pleasure. They are sending out such love because they're happy to see big women looking terrific. Finally, and perhaps most important, you are going to gain self-assurance, beauty secrets, and an experience which will enrich your personal life. Some dreams *do* come true.

What happens if you can't become a model? Well, what happens when a size-six doesn't become a model?

Size alone is not the final criteria for admission into the profession. Neither, for that matter, is great personal beauty. Modeling has definite prerequisites just as acting or any other competitive field has, be it athletics, photography, or any creative endeavor. Technique must be learned. There is also that indescribable "X" factor that makes one person succeed where another fails. In modeling, one woman is photogenic, the other is lackluster. So it goes.

LETTING GO BEFORE THE LENS

Really fine models, to use an old expression, "make love to the camera." They use their faces, their eyes, their bodies. They are incredibly uninhibited. Their concentration is total. What is the difference between the dazzling, handsome college quarterback and Robert Redford—or a top fashion model like Cheryl Teigs and Hollywood High School's Prom Queen? Why is the football player hawking insurance and the prom queen working in a travel agency after graduation while the stars go on and on? It takes that indescribable something, as well as that one big break, as clichéd as it seems.

Even if you don't eventually become a model, why not rejoice that at least now big women do have a *chance* for a dream come true! What's more, because that dream is coming true for a select few BBWs, the rest of us can expect a near century of prejudice against large women eventually to dissipate.

Myth:

ALL THIS BOOK DOES IS GIVE YOU PERMISSION TO BE FAT.

Cleverley Stone a
daughter Kathryn

False.

All this book does is give you permission to be happy and beautiful whatever your size.

Consider this letter:

Dear Carole:

I am enclosing pictures so that you can see what a dramatic change your BBW philosophy has made in my life.

The first picture (I'm sure you'll have no trouble figuring out which one) was taken two years ago. I was truly unhappy about myself and had a terrible self image. But that is obvious in the photo. I was holding my beautiful baby daughter and I couldn't even muster a smile. All I could think about was how terrible this picture was going to be.

*Then, while grocery shopping one day I saw a copy of **BBW Magazine.** On the cover was a beautiful large-size model. She was gorgeous. Her hair and her makeup was just like the cover girls in the other high fashion magazines. It suddenly dawned on me that if she could be pretty, maybe I could too.*

Slowly my own metamorphosis started. I experimented with makeup and hairstyles. I took more pride in the way I dressed. I still wear the same size dress. It just feels better. I feel good about myself for the first time in a long, long, while.

And do you know what? The icing on the cake is that today I am a working model.

Thank you.

Sincerely,
Cleverley Stone
Red Bank, N.J.

16 | ON THE JOB BIGOTRY

It's hard for anyone to learn to cope if he or she is different from everyone else at work. Say you're the only black in the office, or the only Mexican, or the only Jew, or the only one over 60, or the only fat person. You *are* different in some obvious way. It is not a paranoid reaction on your part.

The first and possibly most painful thing you must realize is that no amount of effort will obliterate this difference. If you're the only black person, you're the only black person. What else can you say? All right, now I'm going to be white! Or, say you're handicapped. Barring intervention from above, there's no way you're going to alter your status. If you're fat, unless you decide to undergo the tortures of dieting, you're going to remain that way unless you institute some devious ploy to hook your entire office on chocolate hot fudge sundaes.

Jokes aside, if you are distinctly different weightwise from everyone else at work, you must look the issue squarely in the eye in order to overcome it.

JOB DISCRIMINATION: NOT A JOKE

I wish it were different, but BBWs must realize they invariably will face employment discrimination when looking for work and even after they are hired.

247

Why do people get so hot under the collar if you are fat? I guess the reason is that people think we are the perpetrators of what they consider our "deformity." We are the ones to blame. You can't blame the alcoholic—he's probably suffered a chemical imbalance in his genes. Don't blame the drug addict—circumstances forced that person to crave his daily fix. But you can blame the fat person—after all, if you just shut your mouth you'd be thin like everyone else. Doesn't it sound logical? It begins to when you hear the same damn thing day after day. When enough abuse gets heaped upon us, we start to accept our role as victim. They'll excuse you if you're an alcoholic or a drug addict or a criminal. They'll blame it on your mother or your environment—but if you're a large person, they'll show no mercy whatsoever, apparently feeling no compunction about saying things in the most sarcastic way.

KEEP YOUR GUARD UP

The most familiar type of discrimination large people face is bias during a job hunt.

This discrimination, of course, is concealed. A personnel director may thumb through the photographs of prospective candidates and dismiss all fat people without reading their resumes.

Blatant discrimination occurs when a fat person survives an interview. He or she is qualified in every way, but the company's corporate image prohibits hiring large employees. "Lose 30 lbs.," the interviewer will sometimes say patronizingly, "and we'll be delighted to have you!"

Many times the 'story' is that the company's insurance plan prohibits the hiring of overweight people. Baloney! Most companies with multiple employees have blanket coverage without regard to weight. About all you can do in this case is ask the interviewer to show you the company policy in writing. That way you can either expose him for the liar he is or possibly see if the company is discriminating against large-size persons for a possible law suit. But here, even if you win, you lose. There is no way the job will be yours if the personnel director pegs you as a troublemaker.

I don't know how you handle the bigot who objects to your weight. Maybe you can humor him into hiring you. "Did you intend to pay me by the hour or by the pound?" Yet we all know this situation is no laughing matter.

Fortunately, help is on the way in a few enlightened states. Michigan has already passed a law forbidding discrimination against people because of their size. Maryland tried to legislate similar laws, but a recent bill was shot down when representatives could not agree on a legal definition of obesity without consulting those unreliable height/weight charts. Ohio is currently sponsoring an anti-discrimination bill, which if passed, will provide a model for all other states to emulate.

The bill is the brainchild of Ohio State Senator Michael Schwarzwalder (D-Columbus), who himself is only of average size, but whose paternal side was broadbuilt and large-boned.

Although fervently devoted to the cause of big Americans, Schwarzwalder lamented to me that his colleagues are far from taking the problem seriously. His own interest in sponsoring the bill came from the 120 letters his constituents sent in to affirm their need. He recommends a letter campaign and face-to-face interaction with senators and representatives if BBWs want this bill passed and legislation proposed in other states.

Schwarzwalder, although certain that the category of size will one day uniformly be added to the traditional discrimination categories of sex, national origin, religion and age, cautions that government backing is not a panacea. Schwarzwalder knows full well what every large-size person has learned through one or more unpleasant experiences: Discrimination invariably involves people who are fairly subtle.

However, he does offer the consoling thought that even if a handful of solid cases materialize, employers will be forced to think twice before discriminating against us. Already the senator's work has brought him several clear-cut examples of discrimination which might stand up if brought to court.

In one instance, a friend of Schwarzwalder's was interviewing for an office position at a manufacturing company. Directly ahead of him in line was a large woman who was being interviewed by the recruiter. After she left, the interviewer made a remark that the big woman would never be hired because she was too fat. The job had nothing to do with size, but the interviewer thought that she could blatantly tell Schwarzwalder's friend that she was discriminating, solely because *he* was not a big person. As we all know, enough small-size and regular-size people exist who have a BBW lover, friend or relative, so that at least some of these transgressions will be exposed.

ARE BIG PEOPLE HANDICAPPED

As you may not know, big people are protected under *federal* law, but this is one of those can't-win situations. The law, you see, protects fat persons because it considers us *handicapped*. Federal lawmakers—in a well-meaning but blundering way—have categorized fat people as inferior or incapacitated breed apart from "normal" people.

When the legislators pictured someone "obese," they envisioned a person incapacitated by weight to a degree comparable to a crippling birth defect or blindness.

While of course I am pleased that extremely large persons whose functions are limited by weight are covered, it aggravates me that the majority of active, large women remain helpless when it comes to discrimination by some bigot in a personnel department who is turned off by anyone size 16 or over. I feel like taking every such pea brain by the throat and howling: "You moron! You need a competent person to handle certain tasks, yet you deny a fully qualified person on the basis of a size tag!"

SNIVELING AIN'T THE ANSWER

I'm not talking about the crybabies who swear that everyone is picking on them. There are those people—big people among them—who put the blame for losing out on a job on their physical size, racial origin or some other characteristic when in fact someone else simply was more qualified. We've all heard the story about the stuttering radio announcer who just "c-c-couldn't" understand why he was being passed over.

I am talking about individuals such as a health nurse I know who is a logical, non-inflammatory person. "I have been put up for a promotion many, many times by my immediate superior and turned down each time by the big brass. The reason they gave is that they say I'm 20 to 50 lbs. too heavy. They call me a bad "walking picture" for what is their image of a healthy employee. Yet in one year I have not lost a single day's work, my vital signs are perfect, and my work record is unequaled."

When I speak of discrimination against BBW job applicants and workers, I also exclude anyone who appears as the frumpy, slovenly stereotype that the general public has in mind when they picture a fat woman.

YOU WON'T GET SPECIAL FAVORS

Don't think that the personnel director has any knowledge of what the world is like from a big person's point of view unless she/he is a big person too, or is related to one. They don't know, nor can they be expected to care, that it may be extra difficult for a large-size person to find decent clothes. Do not think you are excused if you go to work or an interview with a stain on your blouse, a run in your stocking, or so forth. No one can expect preferential treatment in a chic advertising agency where the office uniform encompasses wonderful scarves, fine jewelry and classy designerwear, if she stumbles in wearing a polyester polonaise. I mean it *is* reasonable for an employer to expect you to fit into the office environment where dress style is concerned.

On the other hand, every BBW employee and job applicant should learn how to handle discrimination cases as well as possible. When it comes to fighting back at this stage, we're clearly number two or even number three. There is much that we can learn from women, blacks, Chicanos and minorities of every stripe if we're going to become pros at eliminating bigotry.

DO YOUR HOMEWORK

A job prospect who is large is going to have to dazzle the interviewer with her footwork. Learn as much as possible about the company of your choice beforehand. As an employer myself, I can tell you it rates high when an applicant discusses my product in a knowledgeable way. If you cared enough to prepare for this interview, it suggests you'll later care about your job. Another plus comes when you look your interviewer right in the eye to provide your undivided attention. Be prepared to answer the *expected* questions about your personal goals, work history and why you want the job. Exude confidence, though not arrogance, as you discuss your ability to do the job and benefit the company. You may want to check out your local library for books that deal with job interviews and preparation of resumes.

YOU CAN'T, UNFORTUNATELY, WIN 'EM ALL

What do you do, if after all your fancy footwork, homework and preparation, you are still stopped short because the interviewer objects to your size? Or, what if you get the job and you face the tyranny of some superior who lords it over anyone who is large-sized?

How I wish in one exquisitely constructed paragraph I could give you a foolproof method for overcoming prejudice against weight. I can't give you the answer, nor will Senator Schwarzwalder, experts in personnel, or successful BBW job applicants. We are dealing with the objective (your skills and experience), the subjective (the interviewer's prejudice against weight), and the non-objective (an interviewer might not like you personally if you weighed 108 lbs. soaking wet).

GET YOUR FOOT IN THE DOOR

I have one suggestion—one that I realize may offend some people who'll mutter, "But why should we *have* to!" First of all, let me say that I am a realist. I believe that some questions have no logical or digestible answers. They simply exist. One can waste time ranting about the slings and arrows of outrageous fortune, but I always prefer to make a realistic (as opposed to theoretical) attempt to solve my problems.

Therefore, if it is a job you really, really want and need, if you feel in your heart that your talent will overcome initial prejudice and make you nearly indispensable—offer to take the position at a reduced salary or deferred pay for a specific period of time—even offer to do it without pay. I've done it myself. When I was a young singer, I worked for free to get the chance to succeed. I felt in my heart that I would do so well that I would then be offered the job for a fair and steady income. People in the arts frequently work for nothing or low wages to get their foot in the door. The same thing can work in more traditional professions.

A former pro football player with no other experience, went to the Smith Pipe Company of Houston—the nation's seventh largest black-owned business—and worked six months to learn the business without earning a dime. At the end of six months, he was given the job. Three months after that, he was made corporate vice president. Sometimes you *can* beat the system.

TAKE A CHANCE

Sure it hurts to think of a person with years of solid experience and education being forced to work for less-than-deserved compensation because of a weight factor, but at least you are reacting in a way that may counteract the interviewer's bigotry. Because he is getting a bargain by getting your time for free or next-to-nothing, the bigoted interviewer will get the benefit of seeing you in action. Your skill and aplomb may win him over yet.

If you can tell by the interviewer's body language that you don't have a shot in hell at this job, what can you do? You can get up, mumble polite thanks, and then skulk off—or you can take advantage of the fact that this job's been blown anyway and use the opportunity to nail a bigot to the nearest rafter.

Let's say you do decide to put a bigot in his place. How? Do you insult him or show anger? Do you make him confront his prejudice? Do you take him to a higher up or find out if the company has an equal opportunity officer?

Do you turn around and say: "Please correct me if I'm wrong, but the message I've been getting from you is that if I typed 90 words per minute, took shorthand at 120, and had better experience than any other applicant, I couldn't get this job on a bet because I'm fat. Now if I *am* right, will you please give me the courtesy of telling me?"

BRING THINGS TO A HUMAN LEVEL

Maybe this is the opportunity to say: "I want to ask you something off the record. Is there anybody in your family or your sphere of friends who is a large-size person? Anyone that you love in particular?" Now, nobody can say, "I don't know *any* large-size people!" That would be impossible. So when they concede that they do, say: "Wouldn't you hire them? I mean, I can tell that you're not used to the way *I* look, but what would happen to *them* if they were confronting an interviewer with your attitudes for a job?" You've nothing to lose, so throw in your clincher. "Would you at least grant me the courtesy of rethinking my application for a few minutes?"

If nothing else, you've personalized the situation, bringing a human touch to this bigot whose character flaw may hopefully be more steeped in ignorance than malice. Another idea might be to ask him to tell you what went wrong during the interview. This may throw him offstride or may give you a valuable tip about something *you* really are doing wrong. "I don't want to make the same mistake in another interview I have coming up!" is certainly an innocent enough comment to make.

If, on the other hand, someone rudely tells you to get your fat ass on out of there, you can tell him you're actually an undercover reporter for a great metropolitan newspaper. Or you may smile sweetly and say: "I may or may not lose my weight, but you'd better start worrying about your job. I am reporting you to your superiors, as well as the appropriate government agencies."

When all is said and done, after you've let off a bit of steam or simply made an attempt to retain your dignity, the fact remains that there you are—without a job. I feel for your frustration. What can I do to ease the frustration when talent and charisma are ignored by someone who is locked into external evaluations? The advice you're used to hearing is to tell *you* to change. I really don't think that solution is either advisable or realistic in the long run.

What if you do lose six sizes in the next six months, go back to see that bigoted interviewer, and he gives you the job? You've won a Pyrrhic victory at best. In your heart of hearts you won't feel like you've won, perhaps because you've sold out to another's prejudices.

There are others in the boat with you. There are others fighting back both actively and passively. We can't make the other side walk a mile in our pantihose to see how we feel, but slowly and surely we are forming a united front.

IT'S THE LAW

Jim Horn, Assistant Director for the Michigan Department of Civil Liberties, points out that relatively few people (less than half of one percent of all caseloads) have availed themselves of their privilege to lodge a complaint for weight discrimination. However, of the 78 cases logged between 1976 and 1980, some significant reversals against height/weight proportions have been won against law enforcement and security guard companies. The reason for the extremely low complaint number, says Horn, is that so few people *overtly* discriminate against large people.

If you live in Michigan, where legal resource is available, or if you decide to go through federal or individual company channels, Horn has some advice. First of all, document everything provable against the person or persons discriminating against you. Save any memoranda, written communications, and other forms of paperwork which demonstrate bias in black-and-white. Keep a daily diary to record verbal instances of bias. Begin looking for witnesses who can corroborate your story; otherwise, it's often a case of your word against theirs. Be alert to the fact that once a suit is filed, you as the accuser are subject to extremely close scrutiny in all areas of your job and even personal life. Save all commendations and make a written note of all instances where a superior praises your performance. You must also report all transgressions through company channels *first*—even if nothing is done.

You'll need similar record-keeping if you plan on filing a civil suit with the Equal Employment Opportunities Commission. They will conduct an investigation, and if your allegations are provable, they will prosecute an offender.

A woman recently won a case against a major airline that fired her because she weighed 160 lbs. on a 5'6" frame. This woman's victory helps make the public aware that BBWs no longer are willing to tolerate discrimination in the working world.

I wish I could just reach out to right all the wrongs being done to qualified, talented people simply because they cast a bigger shadow than a recruiter or employer.

There is one consolation, and here I am paraphrasing a very wise old black Houston businessman who runs a $50-million-a-year operation supplying pipes for the oil industry—a profession dominated by white interests. Whenever he walks into a situation where he is denied a business contract solely on the basis of his color, he looks that man in the eye and says: "You can deny me because of how I look, but I'll tell you something. *Your* son won't deny *my* son. If he does, your grandson won't deny my grandson. Somewhere along the route, all your hatred and prejudice is going to fade away with your memory. And thank God, there's nothing you can do to stop it!"

A wise man! I don't think I could put it any better. One day we too shall overcome!

17 | SNAPPY COMEBACKS TO DUMB CRACKS

One day after finishing a mid-afternoon fashion show in Southern California, I stopped off for a late lunch at an elegant restaurant with six or seven gorgeous big models. When we entered, a good-looking fellow jumped up from his seat with a smile of greeting and held open the door for us. It was a nice gesture. Then his fashionably thin lady friend took a look at us and said aloud, "Jeee-sus!" in a tone which left unspoken the last words: "Did you ever see so many cows in your life?"

We all heard it and stiffened. But the last model through the door turned and walked back, bending down to look face to face at the girl. "I get $100 an hour to look like this," she challenged. "How much do *you* get for looking the way you look?"

My day was made. The girl's face had sunk so low that we had to step over it to avoid it. Her need to demean and insult us simply because we were fat and she was thin had backfired on her. I only wish that every large-size woman who has ever been callously hurt by some foolish person could have been there that moment.

People who are horrified at the thought of social injustice, people who probably ordinarily wouldn't hurt a fly, think nothing of being rude to a fat person. What gives them permission? Your size and only your size. And *you!* If you let them.

When someone puts you down, it may have little to do with their actual sentiments.

Most likely they could care less about what they're accusing you of—whether they call you fat, skinny, stupid or whatever. They're merely trying to say: "I'm taking control of this situation. I'm making myself more important than you by belittling you." By belittling you and making you less, they're trying to make themselves more, which of course, is a power play that reveals their own insecurities.

When someone puts you down, believe me, it is never to be constructive, no matter how they swear it is so. You must program yourself to call their bluff and master the situation.

There's a famous remark attributed to Orson Welles. A man supposedly said to him: "Orson, you're *fat!*" The great showman responded: "Yes, I *am* fat, but I can diet—*You* are ugly!"

Anyone is entitled to an opinion. People are entitled to view you as pretty, pleasant-looking, unpleasant-looking, old, young, heavy or whatever depending on their own perceptions of things. What they are not entitled to do, however, is to demean you in any way. Nobody!—not your doctor, your lawyer, your spouse, your in-laws—REPEAT—nobody is entitled to demean you!

There are any number of ways of defusing an embarrassing situation depending on your personality and how you want to handle it. But you *do* have to handle it in some way. You can't just stew. You don't have to get emotional; you don't have to grab a celery stalk and stab anyone in the heart; but you don't have to take abuse either.

With someone not so close, but someone you must see frequently, there are several things you can say: "You're overstepping your bounds!"—"Did you intend to be rude or were you just not thinking?"—or "Do you really expect me to answer a cruel remark like that in an even tone of voice?"

In the final category—the most bothersome of all—are repeat offenders, strangers and complete nincompoops who tred upon you because of your weight. For these a good snappy comeback is the way to put them back into their hole where they belong.

Here's some comebacks to frequently heard lines. You may use them or peruse them. You may take them seriously—or just for fun.

CHOW HOUNDING

You're in a restaurant, savoring every morsel on your plate. Savoring it, that is, until a dinner companion (who has ordered the diet special) says, "Are you going to eat all *that?*"

"Nope, I'm a pop sculptor," you say, picking up your fork. "I piled it up to exhibit it in my studio."

The waiter has just brought you dessert when a "friend" across the table says, "Do you really want that?"

After tasting the first bite, you look up and say thoughtfully, "Frankly, I was hoping for something even richer. But this will do for now."

You have just gotten your third raise in six months. Instead of congratulating you, your cousin says, "Doesn't your mouth ever complain about all the stuff you shove into it?"

And, in all honesty you reply, "No more so than yours when you put your foot into it all the time."

WITH FRIENDS LIKE THESE!!!

And then there's the friend who thinks she has all the answers to the world's problems and doesn't mind creating a new problem for you. "Has anyone told you how fat you're getting?" she inquires.

"Of course not," you say. "A friend like you comes along once in a lifetime!"

This person is also likely to smart remark: "Don't you think you should watch your weight?"

Your reply is to the point. "Why should I? You're obviously doing a splendid job of watching it for me."

or

"I'll bet you can't even see the floor when you look down."

"So what," you reply. "When you've seen one floor, you've seen them all!"

or

"If you ask me, I think you ought to lose a couple of pounds."

What simpler answer to that than, "Fair enough. When I want your opinion, I'll ask for it."

THERE OUGHTA BE A LAW

You're dressed to the teeth in a crowded department store when you hear your name called, followed by a shout that makes even your toes wince. "Wow! Have you gained weight!"

"Yes, it *has* been a long time," you shout back in an equally loud voice. "When did you get out of jail?"

By the way, the late Joan Blondell had a wonderful reply to that same tasteless remark about gaining weight. "It's the expensive dress I'm wearing, dearie," she once remarked. "By the way, how come you're looking like that? Is it Halloween?"

★ ★ ★

Walking down the street you're spotted by one of your least favorite people. "Put on a few pounds, I see," says Sarah Sly.

"Darn!" You whisper. "I was hoping you wouldn't recognize me. I don't really want to be seen with you."

HEAVY DUTY COMEBACK

In a *BBW* interview, comedian Avery Schreiber revealed his pat answer to those who say, "You carry your weight well."

With all the sarcasm he can muster, Avery replies: "What did you think I'd do with it? Fall down?"

THEN PUT HIM BACK UNDER HIS ROCK

You're introduced to a tall, dark handsome man with Twinkie cream for a brain. "I'd make love to you," he says, "but you're pretty fat."

"Thank you. I wasn't nearly this pretty skinny!"

or

Him: "If you were my wife, I'd kill you for getting so fat."
You: "If I were your wife, I'd have committed suicide long ago."

or

Him: "You sure let yourself go."
You: "Right! And here I go again. Permanently."

or

Him: "A man like me doesn't like big women."
You: "A big woman like me doesn't consider you much of a man."

or

Him: "I liked you better thin."
You: "I liked *you* better when I was thin too."

or

Him: "I could love you if you were 20 lbs. thinner."
You: "Oh no you couldn't. I'll never let you get that close to me now or ever again."

TURNABOUT IS FOUL PLAY

The salesgirl looks you over critically as you try on a new blouse. "Too bad," she clucks. "You have such a pretty face."

"What's *really* too bad," you reply, "is that you just lost a customer!"

WHEN OLD ACQUAINTANCE SHOULD BE FORGOT

You're in a restaurant out for a night on the town when you spot a classmate you haven't seen in years. "My God!" she says, apparently confusing your name. "I think it's time you dropped 30 lbs."

"Actually, I was thinking of dropping about 135 lbs. . . .*YOU!*"

NOT FUNNY YOU SHOULD SAY THAT

You're at a party when someone tells a joke that makes you howl with glee. In the middle of your laugh, you hear some loudmouth throw out this nasty remark: "Why are fat people so jolly?"

You keep your smile and composure while looking the jerk right in the eye. "They hope that nice people will gravitate toward them instead of people like you."

or

Over the hors d'oeuvres a bon vivant introduces himself by saying. "My you're fat!".

You end the conversation with, "I may be fat—but you're doing a fine job of wearing my patience thin."

or

In the powder room one of the "girls" turns from her giggling friends and sweetly asks, "What's it like to be fat?"

You answer just as sweetly. "What's it like to be rude?"

261

GONE WITH THE WINDBAG

A friend, with nothing better to do with her time than diet, stops you in your tracks. "Want to hear how I lost 20 lbs.?"

"Only if you don't mind boring me to death," you yawn.

or

"Want to hear how many pounds I lost?"

"Sure! If you let me talk about a subject that you find equally boring."

BOOR RELATIONS

Your long forgotten uncle comes in for a visit. "How come you're so fat?" he barks, a big stogie jammed between his teeth.

"Good income, gourmet cooking and great taste," you sniff.

"Are you watching your weight?" Auntie Jo says, patting your tummy.

"Oh no," you confess. "Since I'm making so much money now, I hired someone to keep an eye on it for me!"

Your fourth cousin, three times removed, greets you by saying, "Still have your baby fat, I see."

"Nope, it's full grown fat. So please speak to me with the respect you'd give an adult."

HOT AIR SUNDAE

"I've got just the diet for you," gushes your size four friend as the waitress brings over a menu.

"Tell me about it over dessert," you smile, putting an end to that conversation.

TAKE THIS JIBE AND SHOVE IT

"Do you have a weight problem?" the fresh new kid at work asks to start off your day.

"Yep," you reply, keeping your temper under control. "People come up and make stupid remarks about it."

YOUR CHEATING ARTICHOKE HEART

You're at lunch munching away on lettuce and cottage cheese, pretending that it's a pot roast. Your size six friend watches you impale a tomato slice with your fork. "Do you cheat on your diet?" she suddenly demands.

"Sure," you say, not missing a bite. "And now that we're getting personal, do you cheat on your husband?"

ABBY'S ROADBLOCK

Abigail van Buren has a standard reply to folks who point blank ask how much you weigh. "I'll forgive you for asking," says Dear Abby, "if you'll forgive me for not answering."

BIG DEAL

With all the apparent solicitation in the world, a friend pats you solemnly on the hand and gives you moose eyes. "Have you decided what to do about your weight?" she murmurs.

"Yes," you whisper back, "I decided to keep it."

or

"How could you let yourself go like this?"

"I always go on a binge after I've been attacked by a bore."

or

"Does your husband/boyfriend ever wonder why you're so fat?"

"No. But he did ask me why I hang around with you."

ILL ADVISED

"All that weight isn't good for you," says your friend Josie, who thinks she's a medical expert because she worked as a doctor's receptionist seven years ago.

"Neither is listening to you tear me down," you reply, ending that conversation before it further deteriorates.

★ ★ ★

"Talk about *fat!*" You overhear on your way back to your seat at the theatre.

"All right," you say as you stop, "I'll give you a lecture on what happens to people who make fun of fat people."

PARTING SHOTS

In case someone lashes out with an insult, any insult, here are several "one size fits all" comebacks:

—I'd try to change your mind, *if* I could find it.

—Since you've been nice enough to tell me what's wrong with me, let me tell you what's wrong with you.

—Do you run an insult service, or is this just a hobby with you?

—Do you have any other career ambitions—aside from being God?

—Why is it narrow minds usually have such big mouths?

—If you don't view me as a project for rehabilitation, I won't view you as a pest to be gotten rid of.

—When someone gives me perfect advice I take it. However, neither you nor your advice is anywhere near that.

Don't be surprised if someday, someplace, when you least expect it, you will suddenly remember one of these comebacks at exactly the perfect moment! When that happens, please write and let me know.

TEN STEPS TO A NEW YOU

(WITHOUT LOSING A POUND!)

I wish I had a magic wand to transform society back to the days when a big woman was the epitome of beauty and success. If only there were a secret formula to put into the drinking water of society to alter media-acquired biases against big people! I wish, I wish, I wish, but of course, that's not possible.

Take heart. Having said the negative obvious, I now urge you to join me in working to achieve an altered state with the person nearest, dearest and closest to you. Who? YOU!

STEP ONE: *Look in the mirror!* Resist the temptation to compare yourself to Suzanne Somers, and ask yourself: Exactly what is ugly about my size?

I think you will be surprised at the answer. Yes, you see the stomach and the roll (or rolls) around the middle, but is it *really* unpleasant . . . or do your hands like the feel of the softer, more pliant flesh—all the curves and yes, the crevices? You see?—If it's not unpleasant to your touch, why would it be to another human's touch?

STEP TWO: *Write down at least three wonderful things about yourself.* Be immodest; no one need see your list. Then add at least one more wonderful thing about yourself each day for a week. If you've never been permitted to think of yourself as wonderful, you now have permission in writing.

STEP THREE: *Count your blessings.* You have many, many qualities that make you an outstanding human being. There are talents that you use (or maybe haven't used yet) that make you a worthwhile person. Stop emphasizing the negative and look for your positive traits. List them from one to ten (or even one to 20) on a sheet of paper. Put the list up on your refrigerator door instead of the derogatory signs other big people are told to display there.

STEP FOUR: *Write an obituary for yourself.* Scan several obituaries of famous people in *Time Magazine* or in some major newspaper. Among all their many accomplishments, is there ever a sentence that reads: *He or she stayed thin as a rail?* Of course not. Why? Because in the greater scheme of things, weight has no importance. When you write an obituary you'll be forced to concentrate on what *you* really want out of life—not what some quack dietmonger-book-peddler wants.

STEP FIVE: *Tell yourself that it is all right to get angry at those who try to limit you because of weight.* Anger is a healthy emotion that we big people too often hold back from those who truly deserve it. Make a list of those who anger you because of your weight. It could be a celebrity, a news media person, your neighbor, whatever. Now, *write* each of these people a letter explaining your anger and list specifically their offenses which make you feel as you do. Whether you send them off is up to you (I would!), but now that you've gotten the anger out of your system, on to other things.

STEP SIX: *Allow yourself one full hour a day to worry, indulge in self-pity and grumble about your weight.* "What kind of suggestion is this?" you're probably saying. "Why should I waste a whole hour daily making myself miserable?" I'd have to agree, of course. I'd rather spend that time meditating, swimming, smooching or taking a bubble bath.

If you are spending time already wallowing in remorse and guilt over your weight, this one hour a day beats hell out of many wasted hours and sleepless nights. Soon you'll realize how silly you are being when you plunge yourself into emotional quicksand, and you'll be on your way to a life free from self-imposed constraints.

STEP SEVEN: *Take a snapshot of yourself.* You need a cohort who must promise not to say a word. Take it with our outfit belted; take it unbelted. Take it with your blouse out and tucked in. You can be honest. Don't make up your mind before you see the photo. (Do the same thing when you buy a dress that you're not sure of. Take it home and take a picture.) A Polaroid can be the best friend you have in telling you the truth about how you look. Forget about seeing a fat lady in the picture. Say to yourself before you take the photo: "I am a big woman. A big woman is not a bad woman. Big and bad are not the same thing. A big woman is not an ugly woman, nor are big and ugly the same thing.

STEP EIGHT: *Go through your wardrobe with a fine tooth comb:* Forget sentimentality. Open up your closet and take a long, long look. Are there any clothes in there that resemble the fat lady's traditional outfit? Throw them out! Are there any clothes which make you blue when you wear them? Throw them out! Are there any clothes that depress you because they are left over from the days when you were a size ten? Throw them out. Even if you decide to diet and become a size ten again, those clothes will be too out-of-date to wear. In the meantime, why punish yourself with their presence?

STEP NINE: *Give your home a good housekeeping.* No, I don't mean clean the floors. Nope, your windows are fine. What I want you to do is to throw out all those unpleasant reminders of weight—from your bathroom scale to your calorie counter wristwatch. Yep, box them up good. Seal them tight. You'll see. Your life will go on nicely without them. You've just removed a big source of guilt from your day-to-day living.

STEP TEN: *Live as though you have but one year to live.* Just imagine how you'd feel if some ambassador from an ethereal world came in and said your whole world shuts down for good in 365 days. There's nothing you can do about it, sweetie, except live your life exactly as you want to.

One year—no more. What would you do? Would you diet? I hardly think so. With one year to live you might try some Eggs Benedict for breakfast. Do you think you might forget about your weight and have a little fun, take a few chances, and in general, rearrange your life to get the most out of it? You know you would. 365, 364, 363—*What are you waiting for?*

THE BBW's
TEN
COMMANDMENTS

At the risk of sounding egotistical, like Moses on Mount Sinai I stand here atop my desk at *BBW* to offer Ten Commandments, which if followed, shall lead us to the Promised Land of Self-Contentment. Please take two tablets, but this time—Thank God—you don't have to lose 50 lbs.

I. THOU SHALT HONOR THYSELF FIRST. Stop feeling guilty. You've done nothing wrong by being big. Be good to yourself from now on and give yourself permission to be beautiful.

II. THOU SHALT REJECT THE FALSE GODS OF THINNESS. Let the media, entertainment world and society babble on and on *ad nauseum* about thin being the straight and narrow path to happiness. It's only a road to frustration. Start a new trail and be content.

III. THOU SHALT STOP REHEARSING YOUR LIFE AND LIVE IT. Sure it's nice to perfect yourself as you go, but too many women keep from *doing* anything important because they are always setting up far distant goals. It's time to take advantage of the here and now. If a Prince Charming, a windfall or a career break is going to come, terrific! In the meantime, you are alive right now. Don't blow it. Don't wait in the wings indefinitely no matter what the reason. We don't own time. We are at its mysterious mercy. Time moves—even if you won't!

IV. THOU SHALT HONOR THY FATHER, MOTHER, FAMILY, LOVER, CHILDREN AND FRIENDS, BUT THEY MUST KEEP THEIR MOUTHS SHUT ABOUT YOUR WEIGHT. No one, but no one, has a right to tell you what to do with your life. They may have given you life and been part of the shaping of your life so far, but from now on, it's a whole new ballgame with you in control of yourself. Tell 'em all, lovingly, to leave you the hell alone.

V. THOU SHALT NOT KILL THYSELF WITH FAD DIETS. If you ever want to diet again, fine. If you don't, fine. Never again endanger your health and well-being by following madly to the nearest bookstore to purchase the next "miracle" diet that comes along. A doctor's name on the credit page is no indication of the diet's credibility. *Consumer Guide* has long been a watchdog against foolish weight loss plans. Get a copy of its book, "Rating the Diets," and heed its advice.

VI. THOU SHALT ABANDON ALL HANGUPS ABOUT WEIGHT NO MATTER HOW DEEPLY INGRAINED. Madison Avenue shells out millions to create women in its own image and likeness. But no matter how many times it is repeated, hype is just that— hype. Sure, everywhere you look there are reminders that this is a thin-conscious society, but this is also a society overwhelmed with neuroses, guilt and desperate need for love. Millions of people have been convinced that only starvation, deprivation and self-torture will help them attain love and happiness. Now be honest. Do you really think all thin people are happy?

VII. THOU SHALT NOT STEAL ANY OPPORTUNITIES FOR HAPPINESS AWAY FROM YOURSELF BECAUSE OF WEIGHT. With very few physical exceptions, any profession, occupation and field of physical endeavor has big people in its ranks. There are big entertainers, singers, actors, authors, artists, politicians, businesspeople, professors, laborers, and even at long last models. Reach for the top.

VIII. THOU SHALT NOT LIE TO ANYONE AGAIN ABOUT HOW YOU REALLY FEEL ABOUT YOUR WEIGHT. In the weeks and months to come, some thoughtless persons are going to bring up your weight. In the past you might have said, "I'm planning to go on a diet next week!"—even though you've already been on one for 12 years. Or, you'll apologize, make up excuses, and do anything to cover up how bad this person's comments make you feel. Assert yourself. Say what's on your mind. If this person takes things the wrong way, it just makes the two of you even-steven.

IX. THOU SHALT NOT COVET THY NEIGHBOR'S WIFE. Stop comparing yourself to the woman next door or to the deodorant models on television. You are *you!* Unique, wonderful and exciting. If God wanted to make you like the size-six over the fence, he would have given her a twin.

X. THOU SHALT DARE TO BE A BIG BEAUTIFUL WOMAN. There we have it in a nutshell. It's time that the unthinkable was thought, the unutterable spoken. A big woman can be a beautiful woman if she strives to become so. You owe it to yourself to be as well-dressed, well-groomed, healthy and happy as you can be. The world is yours, my friend. **STOP WEIGHTING—START LIVING!**

Love,

Carole Shaw